**VGM Professional Resumes Series**

THIRD EDITION

RESUMES

ADVERTISING
CAREERS

With Sample Cover Letters

The Editors of VGM Career Books

VGM Career Books

Chicago   New York   San Francisco   Lisbon   London   Madrid   Mexico City
Milan   New Delhi   San Juan   Seoul   Singapore   Sydney   Toronto

Library of Congress Cataloging-in-Publication Data

Resumes for advertising careers / the editors of VGM Career Books.—3rd ed.
    p.   cm.—(VGM professional resumes series)
  ISBN 0-07-140592-5
  1. Resumes (Employment).   2. Advertising—Vocational guidance.   I. VGM
Career Books (Firm).   II. Series.

  HF5383.R43   2003
  808′.06665—dc21

2002028074

1 2 3 4 5 6 7 8 9 0   QPD/QPD   2 1 0 9 8 7 6 5 4 3

ISBN 0-07-140592-5

McGraw-Hill books are available at special quantity discounts to use as premiums and
sales promotions, or for use in corporate training programs. For more information, please
write to the Director of Special Sales, Professional Publishing, McGraw-Hill, Two Penn
Plaza, New York, NY 10121-2298. Or contact your local bookstore.

This book is printed on acid-free paper.

Contents

Introduction

Your resume is a piece of paper (or an electronic document) that serves to introduce you to the people who will eventually hire you. To write a thoughtful resume, you must thoroughly assess your personality, your accomplishments, and the skills you have acquired. The act of composing and submitting a resume also requires you to carefully consider the company or individual that might hire you. What are they looking for, and how can you meet their needs? This book shows you how to organize your personal information and experience into a concise and well-written resume, so that your qualifications and potential as an employee will be understood easily and quickly by a complete stranger.

Writing the resume is just one step in what can be a daunting job-search process, but it is an important element in the chain of events that will lead you to your new position. While you are probably a talented, bright, and charming person, your resume may not reflect these qualities. A poorly written resume can get you nowhere; a well-written resume can land you an interview and potentially a job. A good resume can even lead the interviewer to ask you questions that will allow you to talk about your strengths and highlight the skills you can bring to a prospective employer. Even a person with very little experience can find a good job if he or she is assisted by a thoughtful and polished resume.

Lengthy, typewritten resumes are a thing of the past. Today, employers do not have the time or the patience for verbose documents; they look for tightly composed, straightforward, action-based resumes. Although a one-page resume is the norm, a two-page resume may be warranted if you have had extensive job experience or have changed careers and truly need the space to properly position yourself. If, after careful editing, you still need more than one page to present yourself, it's acceptable to use a second page. A crowded resume that's hard to read would be the worst of your choices.

Distilling your work experience, education, and interests into such a small space requires preparation and thought. This book takes you step-by-step through the process of crafting an effective resume that will stand out in today's competitive marketplace. It serves as a workbook and a place to write down your experiences, while also including the techniques you'll need to pull all the necessary elements together. In the following pages, you'll find many examples of resumes that are specific to your area of interest. Study them for inspiration and find what appeals to you. There are a variety of ways to organize and present your information; inside, you'll find several that will be suitable to your needs. Good luck landing the job of your dreams!

The Elements of an Effective Resume

An effective resume is composed of information that employers are most interested in knowing about a prospective job applicant. This information is conveyed by a few essential elements. The following is a list of elements that are found in most resumes—some essential, some optional. Later in this chapter, we will further examine the role of each of these elements in the makeup of your resume.

- Heading
- Objective and/or Keyword Section
- Work Experience
- Education
- Honors
- Activities
- Certificates and Licenses
- Publications
- Professional Memberships
- Special Skills
- Personal Information
- References

The first step in preparing your resume is to gather information about yourself and your past accomplishments. Later you will refine this information, rewrite it using effective language, and organize it into an attractive layout. But first, let's take a look at each of these important elements individually so you can judge their appropriateness for your resume.

Heading

Although the heading may seem to be the simplest section of your resume, be careful not to take it lightly. It is the first section your prospective employer will see, and it contains the information she or he will need to contact you. At the very least, the heading must contain your name, your home address, and, of course, a phone number where you can be reached easily.

In today's high-tech world, many of us have multiple ways that we can be contacted. You may list your E-mail address if you are reasonably sure the employer makes use of this form of communication. Keep in mind, however, that others may have access to your E-mail messages if you send them from an account provided by your current company. If this is a concern, do not list your work E-mail address on your resume. If you are able to take calls at your current place of business, you should include your work number, because most employers will attempt to contact you during typical business hours.

If you have voice mail or a reliable answering machine at home or at work, list its number in the heading and make sure your greeting is professional and clear. Always include at least one phone number in your heading, even if it is a temporary number, where a prospective employer can leave a message.

You might have a dozen different ways to be contacted, but you do not need to list all of them. Confine your numbers or addresses to those that are the easiest for the prospective employer to use and the simplest for you to retrieve.

Objective

When seeking a specific career path, it is important to list a job or career objective on your resume. This statement helps employers know the direction you see yourself taking, so they can determine whether your goals are in line with those of their organization and the position available. Normally, an objective is one to two sentences long. Its contents will vary depending on your career field, goals, and personality. The objective can be specific or general, but it should always be to the point. See the sample resumes in this book for examples.

If you are planning to use this resume online, or you suspect your potential employer is likely to scan your resume, you will want to include a "keyword" in the objective. This allows a prospective employer, searching hundreds of resumes for a specific skill or position objective, to locate the keyword and find your resume. In essence, a keyword is what's "hot" in your particular field at a given time. It's a buzzword, a shorthand way of getting a particular message across at a glance. For example, if you are a lawyer, your objective might state your desire to work in the area of corporate litigation. In this case, someone searching for the keyword "corporate litigation" will pull up your resume and know that you want to plan, research, and present cases at trial on behalf of the corporation. If your objective states that you "desire a challenging position in systems design," the keyword is "systems design," an industry-specific, shorthand way of saying that you want to be involved in assessing the need for, acquiring, and implementing high-technology systems. These are keywords and every industry has them, so it's becoming more and more important to include a few in your resume. (You may need to conduct additional research to make sure you know what keywords are most likely to be used in your desired industry, profession, or situation.)

There are many resume and job-search sites online. Like most things in the online world, they vary a great deal in quality. Use your discretion. If you plan to apply for jobs online or advertise your availability this way, you will want to design a scannable resume. This type of resume uses a format that can be easily scanned into a computer and added to a database. Scanning allows a prospective employer to use keywords to quickly review each applicant's experience and skills, and (in the event that there are many candidates for the job) to keep your resume for future reference.

Many people find that it is worthwhile to create two or more versions of their basic resume. You may want an intricately designed resume on high-quality paper to mail or hand out *and* a resume that is designed to be scanned into a computer and saved on a database or an online job site. You can even create a resume in ASCII text to E-mail to prospective employers. For further information, you may wish to refer to the *Guide to Internet Job Searching*, by Frances Roehm and Margaret Dikel, updated and published every other year by VGM Career Books, a division of the McGraw-Hill Companies. This excellent book contains helpful and detailed information about formatting a resume for Internet use. To get you started, in Chapter 3 we have included a list of things to keep in mind when creating electronic resumes.

Although it is usually a good idea to include an objective, in some cases this element is not necessary. The goal of the objective statement is to provide the employer with an idea of where you see yourself going in the field. However, if you are uncertain of the exact nature of the job you seek, including an objective that is too specific could result in your not being considered for a host of perfectly acceptable positions. If you decide not to use an objective heading in your resume, you should definitely incorporate the information that would be conveyed in the objective into your cover letter.

Work Experience

Work experience is arguably the most important element of them all. Unless you are a recent graduate or former homemaker with little or no relevant work experience, your current and former positions will provide the central focus of the resume. You will want this section to be as complete and carefully constructed as possible. By thoroughly examining your work experience, you can get to the heart of your accomplishments and present them in a way that demonstrates and highlights your qualifications.

If you are just entering the workforce, your resume will probably focus on your education, but you should also include information on your work or volunteer experiences. Although you will have less information about work experience than a person who has held multiple positions or is advanced in his or her career, the amount of information is not what is most important in this section. How the information is presented and what it says about you as a worker and a person is what really counts.

As you create this section of your resume, remember the need for accuracy. Include all the necessary information about each of your jobs, including your job title, dates of employment, name of your employer, city, state, responsibilities, special projects you handled, and accomplishments. Be sure to list only accomplishments for which you were directly responsible. And don't be alarmed if you haven't participated in or worked on special projects, because this section may not be relevant to certain jobs.

The most common way to list your work experience is in *reverse chronological order*. In other words, start with your most recent job and work your way backward. This way, your prospective employer sees your current (and often most important) position before considering your past employment. Your most recent position, if it's the most important in terms of responsibilities and relevance to the job for which you are applying, should also be the one that includes the most information as compared to your previous positions.

Even if the work itself seems unrelated to your proposed career path, you should list any job or experience that will help "sell" your talents. If you were promoted or given greater responsibilities or commendations, be sure to mention the fact.

The following worksheet is provided to help you organize your experiences in the working world. It will also serve as an excellent resource to refer to when updating your resume in the future.

WORK EXPERIENCE

Job One:

Job Title _____

Dates _____

Employer _____

City, State _____

Major Duties _____

_____

_____

_____

_____

_____

_____

_____

_____

Special Projects _____

_____

_____

Accomplishments _____

_____

_____

_____

_____

_____

Job Two:

Job Title _____

Dates _____

Employer _____

City, State _____

Major Duties _____

_____

_____

_____

_____

_____

Special Projects _____

_____

_____

Accomplishments _____

_____

_____

_____

_____

_____

_____

Job Three:

Job Title _____

Dates _____

Employer _____

City, State _____

Major Duties _____

_____

_____

_____

_____

_____

_____

Special Projects _____

_____

_____

Accomplishments _____

_____

_____

_____

_____

_____

_____

_____

Job Four:

Job Title _____

Dates _____

Employer _____

City, State _____

Major Duties _____

_____

_____

_____

_____

_____

_____

_____

Special Projects _____

_____

_____

_____

Accomplishments _____

_____

_____

_____

_____

_____

_____

_____

Education

Education is usually the second most important element of a resume. Your educational background is often a deciding factor in an employer's decision to interview you. Highlight your accomplishments in school as much as you did those accomplishments at work. If you are looking for your first professional job, your education or life experience will be your greatest assets because your related work experience will be minimal. In this case, the education section becomes an important means of selling yourself.

Include in this section all the degrees or certificates you have received; your major or area of concentration; all of the honors you earned; and any relevant activities you participated in, organized, or chaired. Again, list your most recent schooling first. If you have completed graduate-level work, begin with that and work your way back through your undergraduate education. If you have completed college, you generally should not list your high school experience; do so only if you earned special honors, you had a grade point average that was much better than the norm, or this was your highest level of education.

If you have completed a large number of credit hours in a subject that may be relevant to the position you are seeking, but did not obtain a degree, you may wish to list the hours or classes you completed. Keep in mind, however, that you may be asked to explain why you did not finish the program. If you are currently in school, list the degree, certificate, or license you expect to obtain and the projected date of completion.

The following worksheet will help you gather the information you need for this section of your resume.

EDUCATION

School One _____

Major or Area of Concentration _____

Degree _____

Dates _____

School Two _____

Major or Area of Concentration _____

Degree _____

Honors

If you include an honors section in your resume, you should highlight any awards, honors, or memberships in honorary societies that you have received. (You may also incorporate this information into your education section.) Often, the honors are academic in nature, but this section also may be used for special achievements in sports, clubs, or other school activities. Always include the name of the organization awarding the honor and the date(s) received. Use the following worksheet to help you gather your information.

HONORS

Honor One _____

Awarding Organization _____

Date(s) _____

Honor Two _____

Awarding Organization _____

Date(s) _____

Honor Three _____

Awarding Organization _____

Date(s) _____

Honor Four _____

Awarding Organization _____

Date(s) _____

Honor Five _____

Awarding Organization _____

Date(s) _____

Activities

Perhaps you have been active in different organizations or clubs; often an employer will look at such involvement as evidence of initiative, dedication, and good social skills. Examples of your ability to take a leading role in a group should be included on a resume, if you can provide them. The activities section of your resume should present neighborhood and community activities, volunteer positions, and so forth. In general, you may want to avoid listing any organization whose name indicates the race, creed, sex, age, marital status, sexual orientation, or nation of origin of its members because this could expose you to discrimination. Use the following worksheet to list the specifics of your activities.

ACTIVITIES

Organization/Activity _____

Accomplishments _____

_____

_____

_____

Organization/Activity _____

Accomplishments _____

_____

_____

_____

Organization/Activity _____

Accomplishments _____

_____

_____

_____

As your work experience grows, your education section and school honors or activities may be reduced to include only your degree and any major honors received. As time goes by, your job performance and the experience you've gained become the most important elements in your resume, which should change to reflect this.

Certificates and Licenses

If your chosen career path requires specialized training, you may already have certificates or licenses. You should list these if the job you are seeking requires them and you, of course, have acquired them. If you have applied for a license but have not yet received it, use the phrase "application pending."

License requirements vary by state. If you have moved or are planning to relocate to another state, check with that state's board or licensing agency for all licensing requirements.

Always make sure that all of the information you list is completely accurate. Locate copies of your certificates and licenses, and check the exact date and name of the accrediting agency. Use the following worksheet to organize the necessary information.

CERTIFICATES AND LICENSES

Name of License _____

Licensing Agency _____

Date Issued _____

Name of License _____

Licensing Agency _____

Date Issued _____

Name of License _____

Licensing Agency _____

Date Issued _____

Publications

Some professions strongly encourage or even require that you publish. If you have written, coauthored, or edited any books, articles, professional papers, or works of a similar nature that pertain to your field, you will definitely want to include this element. Remember to list the date of publication and the publisher's name, and specify whether you were the sole author or a coauthor. Book, magazine, or journal titles are generally italicized, while the titles of articles within a larger publication appear in quotes. (Check with your reference librarian for more about the appropriate way to present this information.) For scientific or research papers, you will need to give the date, place, and audience to whom the paper was presented.

Use the following worksheet to help you gather the necessary information about your publications.

PUBLICATIONS

Title and Type (Note, Article, etc.) _____

Title of Publication (Journal, Book, etc.) _____

Publisher _____

Date Published _____

Title and Type (Note, Article, etc.) _____

Title of Publication (Journal, Book, etc.) _____

Publisher _____

Date Published _____

Title and Type (Note, Article, etc.) _____

Title of Publication (Journal, Book, etc.) _____

Publisher _____

Date Published _____

Professional Memberships

Another potential element in your resume is a section listing professional memberships. Use this section to describe your involvement in professional associations, unions, and similar organizations. It is to your advantage to list any professional memberships that pertain to the job you are seeking. Many employers see your membership as representative of your desire to stay up-to-date and connected in your field. Include the dates of your involvement and whether you took part in any special activities or held any offices within the organization. Use the following worksheet to organize your information.

PROFESSIONAL MEMBERSHIPS

Name of Organization _____

Office(s) Held_____

Activities _____

Dates _____

Name of Organization _____

Office(s) Held_____

Activities _____

Dates _____

Name of Organization _____

Office(s) Held_____

Activities _____

Dates _____

Name of Organization _____

Office(s) Held_____

Activities _____

Dates _____

Special Skills

The special skills section of your resume is the place to mention any special abilities you have that relate to the job you are seeking. You can use this element to present certain talents or experiences that are not necessarily a part of your education or work experience. Common examples include fluency in a foreign language, extensive travel abroad, or knowledge of a particular computer application. "Special skills" can encompass a wide range of talents, and this section can be used creatively. However, for each skill you list, you should be able to describe how it would be a direct asset in the type of work you're seeking because employers may ask just that in an interview. If you can't think of a way to do this, it may be extraneous information.

Personal Information

Some people include personal information on their resumes. This is generally not recommended, but you might wish to include it if you think that something in your personal life, such as a hobby or talent, has some bearing on the position you are seeking. This type of information is often referred to at the beginning of an interview, when it may be used as an "icebreaker." Of course, personal information regarding your age, marital status, race, religion, or sexual orientation should never appear on your resume as *personal information*. It should be given only in the context of memberships and activities, and only when doing so would not expose you to discrimination.

References

References are not usually given on the resume itself, but a prospective employer needs to know that you have references who may be contacted if necessary. All you need to include is a single sentence at the end of the resume: "References are available upon request," or even simply, "References available." Have a reference list ready—your interviewer may ask to see it! Contact each person on the list ahead of time to see whether it is all right for you to use him or her as a reference. This way, the person has a chance to think about what to say *before* the call occurs. This helps ensure that you will obtain the best reference possible.

Chapter 2

Writing Your Resume

Now that you have gathered the information for each section of your resume, it's time to write it out in a way that will get the attention of the reviewer—hopefully, your future employer! The language you use in your resume will affect its success, so you must be careful and conscientious. Translate the facts you have gathered into the active, precise language of resume writing. You will be aiming for a resume that keeps the reader's interest and highlights your accomplishments in a concise and effective way.

Resume writing is unlike any other form of writing. Although your seventh-grade composition teacher would not approve, the rules of punctuation and sentence building are often completely ignored. Instead, you should try for a functional, direct writing style that focuses on the use of verbs and other words that imply action on your part. Writing with action words and strong verbs characterizes you to potential employers as an energetic, active person, someone who completes tasks and achieves results from his or her work. Resumes that do not make use of action words can sound passive and stale. These resumes are not effective and do not get the attention of any employer, no matter how qualified the applicant. Choose words that display your strengths and demonstrate your initiative. The following list of commonly used verbs will help you create a strong resume:

administered	assembled
advised	assumed responsibility
analyzed	billed
arranged	built

carried out	inspected
channeled	interviewed
collected	introduced
communicated	invented
compiled	maintained
completed	managed
conducted	met with
contacted	motivated
contracted	negotiated
coordinated	operated
counseled	orchestrated
created	ordered
cut	organized
designed	oversaw
determined	performed
developed	planned
directed	prepared
dispatched	presented
distributed	produced
documented	programmed
edited	published
established	purchased
expanded	recommended
functioned as	recorded
gathered	reduced
handled	referred
hired	represented
implemented	researched
improved	reviewed

saved	supervised
screened	taught
served as	tested
served on	trained
sold	typed
suggested	wrote

Let's look at two examples that differ only in their writing style. The first resume section is ineffective because it does not use action words to accent the applicant's work experiences.

WORK EXPERIENCE
Regional Sales Manager

Manager of sales representatives from seven states. Manager of twelve food chain accounts in the East. In charge of the sales force's planned selling toward specific goals. Supervisor and trainer of new sales representatives. Consulting for customers in the areas of inventory management and quality control.

Special Projects: Coordinator and sponsor of annual food-industry sales seminar.

Accomplishments: Monthly regional volume went up 25 percent during my tenure while, at the same time, a proper sales/cost ratio was maintained. Customer-company relations were improved.

In the following paragraph, we have rewritten the same section using action words. Notice how the tone has changed. It now sounds stronger and more active. This person accomplished goals and really *did* things.

WORK EXPERIENCE
Regional Sales Manager

Managed sales representatives from seven states. Oversaw twelve food chain accounts in the eastern United States. Directed the sales force in planned selling toward specific goals. Supervised and trained new sales representatives. Counseled customers in the areas of inventory management and quality control. Coordinated and sponsored the annual Food Industry Seminar. Increased monthly regional volume 25 percent and helped to improve customer-company relations during my tenure.

One helpful way to construct the work experience section is to make use of your actual job descriptions—the written duties and expectations your employers had for a person in your current or former position. Job descriptions are rarely written in proper resume language, so you will have to rework them, but they do include much of the information necessary to create this section of your resume. If you have access to job descriptions for your former positions, you can use the details to construct an action-oriented paragraph. Often, your human resources department can provide a job description for your current position.

The following is an example of a typical human resources job description, followed by a rewritten version of the same description employing action words and specific details about the job. Again, pay attention to the style of writing instead of the content, as the details of your own experience will be unique.

WORK EXPERIENCE
Public Administrator I

Responsibilities: Coordinate and direct public services to meet the needs of the nation, state, or community. Analyze problems; work with special committees and public agencies; recommend solutions to governing bodies.

Aptitudes and Skills: Ability to relate to and communicate with people; solve complex problems through analysis; plan, organize, and implement policies and programs. Knowledge of political systems, financial management, personnel administration, program evaluation, and organizational theory.

WORK EXPERIENCE
Public Administrator I

Wrote pamphlets and conducted discussion groups to inform citizens of legislative processes and consumer issues. Organized and supervised 25 interviewers. Trained interviewers in effective communication skills.

After you have written out your resume, you are ready to begin the next important step: assembly and layout.

Chapter 3

Assembly and Layout

A t this point, you've gathered all the necessary information for your resume and rewritten it in language that will impress your potential employers. Your next step is to assemble the sections in a logical order and lay them out on the page neatly and attractively to achieve the desired effect: getting the interview.

Assembly

The order of the elements in a resume makes a difference in its overall effect. Clearly, you would not want to bury your name and address somewhere in the middle of the resume. Nor would you want to lead with a less important section, such as special skills. Put the elements in an order that stresses your most important accomplishments and the things that will be most appealing to your potential employer. For example, if you are new to the workforce, you will want the reviewer to read about your education and life skills before any part-time jobs you may have held for short durations. On the other hand, if you have been gainfully employed for several years and currently hold an important position in your company, you should list your work accomplishments ahead of your educational information, which has become less pertinent with time.

Certain things should always be included in your resume, but others are optional. The following list shows you which are which. You might want to use it as a checklist to be certain that you have included all of the necessary information.

Essential	Optional
Name	Cellular Phone Number
Address	Pager Number
Phone Number	E-Mail Address or Website Address
Work Experience	Voice Mail Number
Education	Job Objective
References Phrase	Honors
	Special Skills
	Publications
	Professional Memberships
	Activities
	Certificates and Licenses
	Personal Information
	Graphics
	Photograph

Your choice of optional sections depends on your own background and employment needs. Always use information that will put you in a favorable light—unless it's absolutely essential, avoid anything that will prompt the interviewer to ask questions about your weaknesses or something else that could be unflattering. Make sure your information is accurate and truthful. If your honors are impressive, include them in the resume. If your activities in school demonstrate talents that are necessary for the job you are seeking, allow space for a section on activities. If you are applying for a position that requires ornamental illustration, you may want to include border illustrations or graphics that demonstrate your talents in this area. If you are answering an advertisement for a job that requires certain physical traits, a photo of yourself might be appropriate. A person applying for a job as a computer programmer would *not* include a photo as part of his or her resume. Each resume is unique, just as each person is unique.

Types of Resumes

So far we have focused on the most common type of resume—the *reverse chronological* resume—in which your most recent job is listed first. This is the type of resume usually preferred by those who have to read a large number of resumes, and it is by far the most popular and widely circulated. However, this style of presentation may not be the most effective way to highlight *your* skills and accomplishments.

For example, if you are reentering the workforce after many years or are trying to change career fields, the *functional* resume may work best. This type of resume puts the focus on your achievements instead of the sequence of your work history. In the functional resume, your experience is presented through your general accomplishments and the skills you have developed in your working life.

A functional resume is assembled from the same information you gathered in Chapter 1. The main difference lies in how you organize the information. Essentially, the work experience section is divided in two, with your job duties and accomplishments constituting one section and your employers' names, cities, and states; your positions; and the dates employed making up the other. Place the first section near the top of your resume, just below your job objective (if used), and call it *Accomplishments* or *Achievements*. The second section, containing the bare essentials of your work history, should come after the accomplishments section and can be called *Employment History*, since it is a chronological overview of your former jobs.

The other sections of your resume remain the same. The work experience section is the only one affected in the functional format. By placing the section that focuses on your achievements at the beginning, you draw attention to these achievements. This puts less emphasis on whom you worked for and when, and more on what you did and what you are capable of doing.

If you are changing careers, the emphasis on skills and achievements is important. The identities of previous employers (who aren't part of your new career field) need to be downplayed. A functional resume can help accomplish this task. If you are reentering the workforce after a long absence, a functional resume is the obvious choice. And if you lack full-time work experience, you will need to draw attention away from this fact and put the focus on your skills and abilities. You may need to highlight your volunteer activities and part-time work. Education may also play a more important role in your resume.

The type of resume that is right for you will depend on your personal circumstances. It may be helpful to create both types and then compare them. Which one presents you in the best light? Examples of both types of resumes are included in this book. Use the sample resumes in Chapter 5 to help you decide on the content, presentation, and look of your own resume.

Special Tips for Electronic Resumes

Because there are many details to consider in writing a resume that will be posted or transmitted on the Internet, or one that will be scanned into a computer when it is received, we suggest that you refer to the *Guide to Internet Job Searching*, by Frances Roehm and Margaret Dikel, as previously mentioned. However, here are some brief, general guidelines to follow if you expect your resume to be scanned into a computer.

- Use standard fonts in which none of the letters touch.

- Keep in mind that underlining, italics, and fancy scripts may not scan well.

- Use boldface and capitalization to set off elements. Again, make sure letters don't touch. Leave at least a quarter inch between lines of type.

- Keep information and elements at the left margin. Centering, columns, and even indenting may change when the resume is optically scanned.

- Do not use any lines, boxes, or graphics.

- Place the most important information at the top of the first page. If you use two pages, put "Page 1 of 2" at the bottom of the first page and put your name and "Page 2 of 2" at the top of the second page.

- List each telephone number on its own line in the header.

- Use multiple keywords or synonyms for what you do to make sure your qualifications will be picked up if a prospective employer is searching for them. Use nouns that are keywords for your profession.

- Be descriptive in your titles. For example, don't just use "assistant"; use "legal office assistant."

- Make sure the contrast between print and paper is good. Use a high-quality laser printer and white or very light-colored 8½-by-11-inch paper.

- Mail a high-quality laser print or an excellent copy. Do not fold or use staples, as this might interfere with scanning. You may, however, use paper clips.

In addition to creating a resume that works well for scanning, you may want to have a resume that can be E-mailed to reviewers. Because you may not know what word processing application the recipient uses, the best format to use is ASCII text. (ASCII stands for "American Standard Code for Information Exchange.") It allows people with very different software platforms to exchange and understand information. (E-mail operates on this principle.) ASCII is a simple, text-only language, which means you can include only simple text. There can be no use of boldface, italics, or even paragraph indentations.

To create an ASCII resume, just use your normal word processing program; when finished, save it as a "text only" document. You will find this option under the "save" or "save as" command. Here is a list of things to *avoid* when crafting your electronic resume:

- Tabs. Use your space bar. Tabs will not work.

- Any special characters, such as mathematical symbols.

- Word wrap. Use hard returns (the return key) to make line breaks.

- Centering or other formatting. Align everything at the left margin.

- Bold or italic fonts. Everything will be converted to plain text when you save the file as a "text only" document.

Check carefully for any mistakes before you save the document as a text file. Spell-check and proofread it several times; then ask someone with a keen eye to go over it again for you. Remember: the key is to keep it simple. Any attempt to make this resume pretty or decorative may result in a resume that is confusing and hard to read. After you have saved the document, you can cut and paste it into an E-mail or onto a website.

Layout for a Paper Resume

A great deal of care—and much more formatting—is necessary to achieve an attractive layout for your paper resume. There is no single appropriate layout that applies to every resume, but there are a few basic rules to follow in putting your resume on paper:

- Leave a comfortable margin on the sides, top, and bottom of the page (usually one to one and a half inches).

- Use appropriate spacing between the sections (two to three line spaces are usually adequate).

- Be consistent in the *type* of headings you use for different sections of your resume. For example, if you capitalize the heading EMPLOYMENT HISTORY, don't use initial capitals and underlining for a section of equal importance, such as <u>Education</u>.

- Do not use more than one font in your resume. Stay consistent by choosing a font that is fairly standard and easy to read, and don't change it for different sections. Beware of the tendency to try to make your resume original by choosing fancy type styles; your resume may end up looking unprofessional instead of creative. Unless you are in a very creative and artistic field, you should almost always stick with tried-and-true type styles like Times New Roman and Palatino, which are often used in business writing. In the area of resume styles, conservative is usually the best way to go.

- Always try to fit your resume on one page. If you are having trouble with this, you may be trying to say too much. Edit out any repetitive or unnecessary information, and shorten descriptions of earlier jobs where possible. Ask a friend you trust for feedback on what seems unnecessary or unimportant. For example, you may have included too many optional sections. Today, with the prevalence of the personal computer as a tool, there is no excuse for a poorly laid-out resume. Experiment with variations until you are pleased with the result.

CHRONOLOGICAL RESUME

Lucas Jackson
2399 S. Division • Grand Rapids, MI 49503
(616) 555-9354
Cell: (616) 555-2819
lucasjackson@xxx.com

Objective

Apply my skills as a content expert to a new challenge with a company focused on quality, dedication, and ingenuity.

Work

1998 to present

Content Strategist, Sonic Consulting, Grand Rapids, MI

Provide digital solutions for clients interested in establishing their presence online. Make recommendations on content assets, third-party content partnerships, and content management systems. Direct copywriters and design teams to fulfill the clients' objectives and create brand strategies.

1996 to 1998

Website Manager, *Crash! Magazine*, Detroit, MI

Directed the online version of *Crash! Magazine* and ensured design and content guidelines of the site followed those of the print version. Coordinated special events to drive traffic to the site resulting in a 75 percent increase in hits over four months. Created and edited content specifically for the site to establish its own identity.

1994 to 1996

Writer, *Digital City Magazine*, Detroit, MI

Researched and wrote articles covering the emerging Internet business and issues that relate to that unique business sector. Interviewed people involved in cutting-edge development on the Web and analyzed the business implications of this unique medium.

Skills

- Intimate familiarity with standard style guides including *AP, Chicago Manual, MLA,* and *Wired.*
- Very knowledgeable in the use and merits of content management systems such as Vignette, ePrise, and BroadVision.
- Uncanny ability to merge creative vision with business objectives to create distinctive and engaging content.

References available upon request.

FUNCTIONAL RESUME

Katrina Parker
1402 Greenbriar Road
Charleston, WV 25304
(304) 555-1704

Applications and Systems Programmer

Credentials

- B.S. in Computer Science—March 1995—University of Michigan; minor in Accounting
- Knowledge of COBOL, FORTRAN, Pascal, C, C Plus, BASIC, CAD/CAM, RPG II, Assembly language #68000, 8086 & 6502, and dBASE
- High level of self-motivation and attention to detail

Job Duties

- Code, test, debug, and maintain programs
- Create program documentation
- Integrate new hardware into existing systems
- Diagnose and correct systems failures
- Maintain monitors, database packages, compilers, assemblers, and utility programs
- Select and modify new hardware and software to company specifications

Achievements

- Designed programs in C Plus for Heritage Bank to coordinate functions of ATM machines
- Purchased new hardware and software for Advantage Publishers, modified equipment to suit company's needs and resolve interoperability issues

Employers

Heritage Bank   June 1999 to Present
Advantage Publishers   March 1996 to June 1999

References

Marta Dalton   Renu Das
Vice President of Finance   Director of Human Resources
Heritage Bank   Advantage Publishers
411 Watkins Street   694 Dale Street
Charleston, WV 25304   Deer Park, NY 11729
(304) 555-2225, Ext. 203   (516) 555-7937

Remember that a resume is not an autobiography. Too much information will only get in the way. The more compact your resume, the easier it will be to review. If a person who is swamped with resumes looks at yours, catches the main points, and then calls you for an interview to fill in some of the details, your resume has already accomplished its task. A clear and concise resume makes for a happy reader and a good impression.

There are times when, despite extensive editing, the resume simply cannot fit on one page. In this case, the resume should be laid out on two pages in such a way that neither clarity nor appearance is compromised. Each page of a two-page resume should be marked clearly: the first should indicate "Page 1 of 2," and the second should include your name and the page number, for example, "Julia Ramirez—Page 2 of 2." The pages should then be stapled together. You may use a smaller font (in the same font as the body of your resume) for the page numbers. Place them at the bottom of page one and the top of page two. Again, spend the time now to experiment with the layout until you find one that looks good to you.

Always show your final layout to other people and ask them what they like or dislike about it, and what impresses them most when they read your resume. Make sure that their responses are the same as what you want to elicit from your prospective employer. If they aren't the same, you should continue to make changes until the necessary information is emphasized.

Proofreading

After you have finished typing the master copy of your resume and before you have it copied or printed, thoroughly check it for typing and spelling errors. Do not place all your trust in your computer's spell-check function. Use an old editing trick and read the whole resume backward—start at the end and read it right to left and bottom to top. This can help you see the small errors or inconsistencies that are easy to overlook. Take time to do it right because a single error on a document this important can cause the reader to judge your attention to detail in a harsh light.

Have several people look at the finished resume just in case you've missed an error. Don't try to take a shortcut; not having an unbiased set of eyes examine your resume now could mean embarrassment later. Even experienced editors can easily overlook their own errors. Be thorough and conscientious with your proofreading so your first impression is a perfect one.

We have included the following rules of capitalization and punctuation to assist you in the final stage of creating your resume. Remember that resumes often require use of a shorthand style of writing that may include sentences without periods and other stylistic choices that break the standard rules of grammar. Be consistent in each section, and throughout the whole resume, with your choices.

RULES OF CAPITALIZATION

- Capitalize proper nouns, such as names of schools, colleges, and universities; names of companies; and brand names of products.

- Capitalize major words in the names and titles of books, tests, and articles that appear in the body of your resume.

- Capitalize words in major section headings of your resume.

- Do not capitalize words just because they seem important.

- When in doubt, consult a manual of style such as *Words into Type* (Prentice-Hall) or *The Chicago Manual of Style* (The University of Chicago Press). Your local library can help you locate these and other reference books. Many computer programs also have grammar help sections.

RULES OF PUNCTUATION

- Use commas to separate words in a series.

- Use a semicolon to separate series of words that already include commas within the series. (For an example, see the first rule of capitalization.)

- Use a semicolon to separate independent clauses that are not joined by a conjunction.

- Use a period to end a sentence.

- Use a colon to show that examples or details follow that will expand or amplify the preceding phrase.

- Avoid the use of dashes.

- Avoid the use of brackets.

- If you use any punctuation in an unusual way in your resume, be consistent in its use.

- Whenever you are uncertain, consult a style manual.

Putting Your Resume in Print

You will need to buy high-quality paper for your printer before you print your finished resume. Regular office paper is not good enough for resumes; the reviewer will probably think it looks flimsy and cheap. Go to an office supply store or copy shop and select a high-quality bond paper that will make a good first impression. Select colors like white, off-white, or possibly a light gray. In some industries, a pastel may be acceptable, but be sure the color and feel of the paper make a subtle, positive statement about you. Nothing in the choice of paper should be loud or unprofessional.

If your computer printer does not reproduce your resume properly and produces smudged or stuttered type, either ask to borrow a friend's or take your disk (or a clean original) to a printer or copy shop for high-quality copying. If you anticipate needing a large number of copies, taking your resume to a copy shop or a printer is probably the best choice.

Hold a sheet of your unprinted bond paper up to the light. If it has a watermark, you will want to point this out to the person helping you with copies; the printing should be done so that the reader can read the print and see the watermark the right way up. Check each copy for smudges or streaks. This is the time to be a perfectionist the results of your careful preparation will be well worth it.

Chapter 4

The Cover Letter

Once your resume has been assembled, laid out, and printed to your satisfaction, the next and final step before distribution is to write your cover letter. Though there may be instances where you deliver your resume in person, you will usually send it through the mail or online. Resumes sent through the mail always need an accompanying letter that briefly introduces you and your resume. The purpose of the cover letter is to get a potential employer to read your resume, just as the purpose of the resume is to get that same potential employer to call you for an interview.

Like your resume, your cover letter should be clean, neat, and direct. A cover letter usually includes the following information:

1. Your name and address (unless it already appears on your personal letterhead) and your phone number(s); see item 7.

2. The date.

3. The name and address of the person and company to whom you are sending your resume.

4. The salutation ("Dear Mr." or "Dear Ms." followed by the person's last name, or "To Whom It May Concern" if you are answering a blind ad).

5. An opening paragraph explaining why you are writing (for example, in response to an ad, as a follow-up to a previous meeting, at the suggestion of someone you both know) and indicating that you are interested in whatever job is being offered.

6. One or more paragraphs that tell why you want to work for the company and what qualifications and experiences you can bring to the position. This is a good place to mention some detail about

that particular company that makes you want to work for them; this shows that you have done some research before applying.

7. A final paragraph that closes the letter and invites the reviewer to contact you for an interview. This can be a good place to tell the potential employer which method would be best to use when contacting you. Be sure to give the correct phone number and a good time to reach you, if that is important. You may mention here that your references are available upon request.

8. The closing ("Sincerely" or "Yours truly") followed by your signature in a dark ink, with your name typed under it.

Your cover letter should include all of this information and be no longer than one page in length. The language used should be polite, businesslike, and to the point. Don't attempt to tell your life story in the cover letter; a long and cluttered letter will serve only to annoy the reader. Remember that you need to mention only a few of your accomplishments and skills in the cover letter. The rest of your information is available in your resume. If your cover letter is a success, your resume will be read and all pertinent information reviewed by your prospective employer.

Producing the Cover Letter

Cover letters should always be individualized because they are always written to specific individuals and companies. Never use a form letter for your cover letter or copy it as you would a resume. Each cover letter should be unique, and as personal and lively as possible. (Of course, once you have written and rewritten your first cover letter until you are satisfied with it, you can certainly use similar wording in subsequent letters. You may want to save a template on your computer for future reference.) Keep a hard copy of each cover letter so you know exactly what you wrote in each one.

There are sample cover letters in Chapter 6. Use them as models or for ideas of how to assemble and lay out your own cover letters. Remember that every letter is unique and depends on the particular circumstances of the individual writing it and the job for which he or she is applying.

After you have written your cover letter, proofread it as thoroughly as you did your resume. Again, spelling or punctuation errors are a sure sign of carelessness, and you don't want that to be a part of your first impression on a prospective employer. This is no time to trust your spellcheck function. Even after going through a spelling and grammar check, your cover letter should be carefully proofread by at least one other person.

Print the cover letter on the same quality bond paper you used for your resume. Remember to sign it, using a good, dark-ink pen. Handle the letter and resume carefully to avoid smudging or wrinkling, and mail them together in an appropriately sized envelope. Many stores sell matching envelopes to coordinate with your choice of bond paper.

Keep an accurate record of all resumes you send out and the results of each mailing. This record can be kept on your computer, in a calendar or notebook, or on file cards. Knowing when a resume is likely to have been received will keep you on track as you make follow-up phone calls.

About a week after mailing resumes and cover letters to potential employers, contact them by telephone. Confirm that your resume arrived and ask whether an interview might be possible. Be sure to record the name of the person you spoke to and any other information you gleaned from the conversation. It is wise to treat the person answering the phone with a great deal of respect; sometimes the assistant or receptionist has the ear of the person doing the hiring.

You should make a great impression with the strong, straightforward resume and personalized cover letter you have just created. We wish you every success in securing the career of your dreams!

Sample Resumes

T his chapter contains dozens of sample resumes for people pursuing a wide variety of advertising jobs and careers.

There are many different styles of resumes in terms of graphic layout and presentation of information. These samples also represent people with varying amounts of education and experience. Use these samples to model your own resume after. Choose one resume, or borrow elements from several different resumes, to help you construct your own.

KARIN M. GILES

4019 West Hoop Road • Hagerstown, Maryland 03394
301/555-8476 • karingiles@xxx.com

EMPLOYMENT GOALS

Seeking an entry-level position in advertising, where I can put my organizational and financial skills to work and gain new knowledge and experience.

EDUCATION

Currently enrolled in advertising evening program at Central Community College. Relevant courses taken include advertising, copywriting, business communications, marketing strategies, and ad sales planning. Basic computer skills also acquired.

WORK EXPERIENCE

Medical Office Manager, Henderson Chiropractic Clinic,
Hagerstown, MD (October 1999 to Present)
Handle all insurance billing, accounts payable and receivable, payroll, daily ledger sheet balancing, patient billings, and medical report preparation. Supervise office staff, schedule appointments, and work effectively in a situation that requires a significant amount of patient contact.

Accounting Clerk, Riddle Press, Hagerstown, MD
(March 1998 to September 1999)
Managed full-cycle bookkeeping, accounts payable and receivable, payroll, shift reports, switchboard operation. Completed computer data entry. Served as receptionist.

Bookkeeper, Dr. Stephen L. Davis, Baltimore, MD
(September 1995 to March 1998)
Full-cycle bookkeeper and office coordinator. Set up financial arrangements for orthodontic patients. Completed bimonthly payroll. Processed statements and insurance billing and was responsible for collections. Scheduled appointments. Served as receptionist.

ADDITIONAL EXPERIENCE

Over 12 years of office experience and customer relations. Typing approximately 65 wpm, 10-key, Covalent computer printer, data entry, multiline switchboard system. Well versed in the workings of Microsoft Office applications. Have professional telephone manner and work well with others.

REFERENCES

Furnished on request.

CAMMY WINTERS
5249 SW 9TH AVENUE • SEATTLE, WA 98006
206/555-2332 • CAMMYWINTERS@XXX.COM • CELL: 206/555-8776

OBJECTIVE
A challenging position in advertising graphic design.

SKILLS
- Extensive experience with typography, layout, pasteup, production, and printing.
- Ability to thoroughly research, organize, and manage projects from concept to completion.
- Ability to communicate effectively with clients, in verbal and written forms.
- Solid working knowledge of Macintosh desktop publishing and graphics software applications including QuarkXPress, Adobe Photoshop, PageMaker, and Acrobat.

EDUCATION AND TRAINING
Washington State University
Bachelor of Fine Arts, Printmaking, 1998

University of Washington
Communications, 1995 - 1996

PROFESSIONAL EXPERIENCE
Union Square Gazette, Seattle, WA
October 1998 - Present
Ad Production Clerk II
All aspects of ad production, including dispatching of ads into system for production, input into computer system for typesetting, layout and pasteup, cutting color, proof-reading, running proofs, taking corrections over the phone or counter, delivery of ads as requested by advertiser, and layout and pasteup of the classified section. Required constant communication with coworkers in the sales and production departments, clear communication with clients, and the ability to meet deadlines.

Old Town Desktop Publishing, Olympia, WA
February 1997 - October 1998
Art Director/Production Manager
Design and production, including typesetting, page layout, pasteup, illustration, and liaison with color house printer.

Graphic Designer
Design, layout, and production for client-specific projects. Experience with Page-Maker, Photoshop, Quark, FreeHand, Word, MacDraw, VersaScan, Illustrator, Persuasion, and CricketGraph.

References and portfolio furnished on request.

BENJAMIN BLACKMORE

P.O. Box 5789   benjaminblackmore@xxx.com
Sioux Falls, SD 57104   605-555-9234

CAREER OBJECTIVE

Seeking a position as advertising manager for a manufacturer.

EXPERIENCE

- Coordinated all aspects of high-level corporate visitations from prospective clients.
- Supervised corporate sales force of 128 sales representatives
  nationwide.
- Directed development of marketing strategies, new product develop-
  ment, and advertising and promotion planning.
- Delivered product demonstrations and presentations.
- Designed and wrote product marketing guides, competitive reports,
  and training materials for field representatives.
- Responsible for software installation, applications support, trou-
  bleshooting, and maintenance for 25 accounts.
- Presented sales demonstrations and provided training and customer
  service for installed accounts.
- Assisted with sales office activities.

WORK HISTORY

Hutchinson Computer Corporation, Sioux Falls, SD, 1995 - present
- Senior Support Specialist, 2000 - present
- Field Marketing Specialist, 1997 - 2000
- System Analyst, 1995 - 1997

Market Systems Corporation, Rapid City, SD, 1987 - 1995
- Customer Support Manager
- Support Analyst

Blackmore & Gwynne, Inc., Minneapolis, MN, 1983 - 1987
- Educational Services Representative
- Sales and Marketing Representative

EDUCATION

University of Minnesota, Minneapolis-St. Paul
- B.S. in Business Administration, 1983
- Minor: Advertising and Marketing

REFERENCES AVAILABLE

TOBY MORRISON

3352 W. Evans Drive
Suncook, New Hampshire
(603) 555-4876   Cell: (603) 555-6723
tobymorrison@xxx.com

EXPERIENCE

- Designed and developed display concepts.
- Illustrated renderings.
- Coordinated computer graphic design orders for client jobs.
- Responsible for inventory control and product distribution.
- Developed concepts and carried them to camera-ready state, production, or actual print.
- Produced graphic work including book covers and program layout.
- Established clientele and maintained customer service.
- Responsible for scheduling, security, customer service, and payroll.

WORK HISTORY

DESIGN ENGINEER, Darvol Corporation, Concord, NH	5/99 to present
DESIGNER, Self-Employed	6/96 to present
SUPPORT STAFF, Traver Gallery, Concord, NH	3/98 to 5/99
MANAGER, Concord Bar and Grill, Concord, NH	5/96 to 3/98

EDUCATION

Bachelor of Arts, Arts Administration, University of New Hampshire 5/98

AFFILIATIONS

Progressive Design Group of New Hampshire
Alpha Lambda, Arts Honorary

SPECIAL SKILLS

Apple Macintosh design applications: Adobe PageMaker, Photoshop, Illustrator, and Acrobat; Apple Scan; Claris CAD; MacDraw; QuarkXPress; Ultra Paint; Virts Walkthrough.

Also familiar with general office applications and similar IBM applications.

References and portfolio available.

PORTER HOLLAND

2442 GALLANT ROAD
CHARLOTTE, NORTH CAROLINA 28215
(704) 555-2856
PORTERHOLLAND@XXX.COM

OBJECTIVE	Seeking a position as media buyer for local ad agency
EDUCATION	Hamline University, St. Paul, MN B.S., Journalism and Advertising June 2001
EXPERIENCE	Directed national advertising print media campaign. Two years of progressively more responsibility in media buying and development of media relations. Ability to handle every aspect of advertising development, from concept to copywriting to design and production. Computer fluent with IBM and Macintosh systems for word processing, graphic design, and page composition utilities. Developed and implemented consumer surveys at point-of-purchase outlets. Assisted research department with compilation and analysis of survey results.
WORK HISTORY	Assistant Media Buyer, Faver-Williams, Inc., Charlotte, NC 2001-Present Advertising Intern, Marshall Fields, Minneapolis, MN Summer and Fall 2000 Research Assistant, Journalism Department, Hamline University, St. Paul, MN, 1997-2000
REFERENCES	Available

Mary E. Glancey

72 College Street • Beloit, Wisconsin 53511
(606) 555-4267 • maryglancey@xxx.com

Objective

To secure a position in advertising copywriting

Education

Beloit College, Beloit, Wisconsin
Bachelor of Arts in Journalism, expected June 2003
Minors in Creative Writing and Multicultural Studies

Honorable Mention, Thorpe Prize for Creative Writing, 2000

Relevant Courses: Journalism, Advertising Writing, Campaign Management and Strategic Planning, Advertising Account Management, Business Communications, and Creative Writing.

Computer Skills

On Macintosh and IBM-PC computers, have working knowledge of the following software: QuarkXPress, MS Word, MacWrite, PageMaker, Photoshop, Acrobat, CricketGraph, FreeHand, Illustrator, Mousewrite, Multiscribe GS, WordPerfect 6.1, and Appleworks.

Supporting Experience

- Served as advertising coordinator for weekly college newspaper, 1999-2001
- Attended Desktop Publishing Workshop for professional training in use of QuarkXPress software program, April 1999
- Worked as copyeditor for college newspaper, fall 1999
- Assisted as copyeditor for professor's philosophy dissertation, 1998
- Contributed as reporter and photographer for college paper, 1998-2000
- Assisted in producing and circulating bimonthly newsletter for the Women's Center, 1998-2000

Additional Experience

Also worked as substitute teacher, child care provider, preschool instructor, restaurant server, cook and busperson, newspaper deliverer, cashier, office aide, caterer, and ski chairlift operator.

College Activities

Active as varsity athlete in softball and soccer, as volunteer with the admissions office, and as an Outing Club member. Member of Students for an Integrated Curriculum and Beloit College Women's Center.

References available on request

Tammy Blakewood

2500 Francisco Blvd. • Pacifica, CA 94044
(415) 555-7833 • Cell: (415) 555-6555 • tammyblakewood@xxx.com

Summary of Qualifications

More than ten years of experience in a position demanding organizational, administrative, and interpersonal skills. Adept at handling situations requiring prompt, tactful decisions. Highly motivated and dependable. Work well with people at all levels.

Experience

Blakewood & Associates, 241060 N. Beach Drive, Pacifica, CA 94045
Owner/Sole Proprietorship
February 1998 - Present

Structured and created desktop publishing and advertising services enterprise, based in a town of approximately 10,000. Primary activities include basic graphic design and laser typesetting for a quick-print shop. Designed and created camera-ready art for a tabloid for the Combined Counties Police Association that consisted of a 24-page, two-color display section and a 20-page editorial section with electronically scanned halftones.

H.H.S. and B. Advertising, 55 Oviedo Court, Pacifica, CA 94044
Operations Manager
March 1995 - February 1998

Originally hired as an entry-level advertising account representative for a small agency. Assumed responsibility for all client reconciliation and billing, personnel scheduling, training and management, print media planning and placement, and outside print production contracting. Gradually developed and maintained efficient office management forms and systems program. Produced print media for publication in the *San Francisco Chronicle*, the *Oakland Tribune*, and the *Wall Street Journal* using desktop publishing. Gained industry experience in radio and television concept, copywriting, and production.

Special Skills

Macintosh and IBM with various software including Quark, PageMaker, Word, Works, Excel, Lotus SmartSuite, Tapscan Media Reach, Fast-Pak Mail, and The Editor.

Education

A.A. in Design, 1998
Pacifica College, Pacifica, CA

References available on request

Karl M. Landon

156 N. 25th Street • Arlington, Texas 75234 • 817-555-8678 • karllandon@xxx.com

■ Career Objective

To create and manage professional, results-oriented advertising in a challenging environment.

■ Education

Bachelor of Science, Journalism/Advertising
Texas Wesleyan University, 1995

■ Skills and Achievements

• Directed national advertising campaigns from concept development to media placement.
• Six years of progressively more responsible experience in managing the in-house advertising agency of an international corporation.
• Ability to handle every aspect involved in publishing a monthly magazine.
• Small staff supervisory experience.
• Bachelor of Science degree with a major in Journalism and a minor in Advertising.
• Computer fluent with IBM and Macintosh systems running word processing and desktop publishing software.

■ Experience

Self-Employed Creative Director, 1999–present
Created an advertising and publications service. Responsible for new business development and managing existing account activity. Publish a monthly 20-page, high-quality magazine for one client. Provide writing, editing, proofing, photography, design, layout, production management, advertising sales, and mailing. Assist on production of a monthly business newspaper. Desktop publishing accounts for 40% of daily activities.

Director of Advertising, Border Burritos, Inc., 1996–1999
Coordinated all national and regional advertising efforts for this 200-store fast-food restaurant chain. Supervised all creative development and broadcast production through an outside agency. Developed all collateral print production. Supervised regional media buying. Created all corporate self-promotion materials.

Media Buyer, Texas Marketing Association, January–November, 1996
Television and radio buyer for the Texas Marketing Association, a 56-store media co-op.

Student Intern, Galigaskan's Sandwiches, June–December, 1995
Media buyer for company-owned restaurants in Arlington; research assistant on regionally constructed image and awareness survey; evaluated all company store sales results from advertising campaigns.

■ Other Activities

Board of Directors, Texas Ad Club
Individual Sponsor, American Advertising Museum
Speaker, 1999 Texas Wesleyan Journalism School Career Day
Award of Excellence and Achievement, Texas Ad Club

—————— **JANE BREEN** ——————

3804 N. Damen #1 • Milwaukee, WI 53201 • 414/555-5616 • janebreen@xxx.com

EMPLOYMENT ——————

1999-present: MAGNAN & ASSOCIATES ADVERTISING
345 North Canal Street, Suite 1402, Milwaukee, WI
Executive Director

Art direction, design, layout, computer graphics, freelance management, and copywriting. Obtain sources for vendors and suppliers. Implement computer graphics systems.
Clients: Schwinn Bicycle Corporation, Rand McNally, TDM, Sassy (baby products), Guarantee Trust Life Insurance, Margie's Bridal.

1998-present: FREELANCE WORK (Milwaukee)
Clients: Beltone (BEC Advertising), Davidson Marketing Services Inc., MB Pasternak Associates, Wooster-Magnani Advertising, Roman Inc.

1994-1999: BREEN GRAPHICS
677 North Racine Street, Chicago, IL
Executive Director

Directed projects from initial client contact through camera-ready art. Concept and strategy development. Design, production, and line and graphic illustration. Contracted for typesetters, camera work, printers, freelance photography, keyline, and illustration. Managed finances.
Clients: WARM 98FM, Spectrum Publishing, Forest View Gardens Restaurant, Kelore International Nailcare, The Creative Factory, I.A. Associates, The Finishing Touch Interiors, Deletext Systems, *The Downtowner* Newspaper, Business Type Services, and the Under 5th Café.

1990-1994: ANTONELLI INSTITUTE OF ART
125 East 7th Street, Cincinnati, OH
Commercial Art Instructor/Advertising Coordinator

Taught Typography, Production Art I & II, Product Illustration, Layout, Graphic Design, Computer Graphics, Corporate Campaign Direction, and Drawing. Created and implemented curriculum changes to incorporate new computer graphics program.

1985-1989: WIII-TV 64
5177 Fishwick Drive, Cincinnati, OH
Art Director

Design and production of all print and outdoor advertising. *TV Guide* and local newspaper ads, billboards and busboards, sales and promotional materials including brochures, contest materials, posters, letterheads, camera cards, storyboards, ad sign painting, news and ID photography. Obtained vendor sources. Worked closely with marketing manager in selecting appropriate advertising vehicles.

EDUCATION ——————

B.F.A. in Fine Arts, with concentration in Graphic Arts
Indiana University, graduated June 1985

References on request

KIMBERLY ANNE MORLEY

753 Elmore Drive
Little Rock, Arkansas 72202

501/555-1047
kimberlymorley@xxx.com

OBJECTIVE

Account executive position with small, independent advertising firm.

EXPERIENCE

Arkansas Sun Times Corporation, Pioneer Publishing Company, Little Rock, AR
Display Advertising Account Executive
1998 - Present
- Service and develop $350,000 territory for 38 suburban weekly newspapers.
- Technical knowledge of advertising, design, prepress, and printing functions.
- Experience in budgeting, pricing strategies, and proposal writing.
- Coordinate local advertising promotions.

Stone Container Corporation, Tempe, AZ
Marketing Coordinator
1997 - 1998
- Coordinated and produced marketing and promotional materials and activities for leading international package company.
- Organized and produced special events.
- Produced quarterly design awards program.
- Designed sales presentations using computer.

EDUCATION

Columbia College, Chicago, IL
B.A. in Liberal Arts, with honors, June 1997

Arizona State University, Tempe, AZ
A.A. in Graphic Arts Processes/Photography, May 1995

REFERENCES

Available upon request.

JOSEPH D. CAROTHERS

98 East 150th Street
Bloomington, IN 42167
812-555-9509
josephcarothers@xxx.com

OBJECTIVE

Traffic Production Manager for an advertising agency or corporate advertising division

EXPERIENCE

- Management of creative efforts and staff operations in graphic arts, illustration, and photography for the publishing and advertising industry.
- Design and layout direction for magazine covers and articles, packaging, TV storyboards, advertising, point-of-sale promotions, brochures, books, posters, direct mail, and displays.
- Supervision of editorial layout, artwork, typography, and production; working with senior management in coordination of production operations and general business functions.
- Staff training and supervision, budget planning, work flow scheduling, and administrative management.
- Direct client services and sales support, vendor evaluation, and contract negotiation.
- Work closely with the sales and marketing staff of advertising agency.
- Supervise freelance illustrators, art directors, and designers on special projects.

EDUCATION

Colorado Institute of Art, B.F.A., June 1989
Advertising Design—Graduated "Top Designer" out of 125

Texas Tech University, A.A., May 1985
Commercial Art, Architectural Design & Construction

School of Modern Photography
Advertising Photography course work, 1998 - 2000

Indiana Institute of Technology
Business Management course work, 1995 - 1998

EMPLOYMENT HISTORY

1998 - Present	Design Marc Advertising, Bloomington, IN	Creative Art Director
1996 - 1998	Amway Corporation, Ada, MI	Supervisor of Advertising
1994 - 1996	Crain Communications, Chicago, IL	Art Director, *Health News*
1989 - 1994	American Bar Association Press, Chicago, IL	Creative Art Director

REFERENCES AVAILABLE

MARGARET M. JANSEN

11 Parkside Lane, No. 265

Salt Lake City, Utah 84116

(801) 555-9863

margaretjansen@xxx.com

EDUCATION

University of Utah
Salt Lake City, Utah
Master of Science in Marketing, 1995

Patterson State College
Ogden, Utah
Bachelor of Sciences in Business, 1982

EMPLOYMENT HISTORY

Marketing/Advertising Director, Guardian State Bank, 1999-Present
- Research target markets and competitive markets
- Prepare complete market plan for introduction of new marketing services
- Design artwork and coordinate production
- Design and prepare in-house art and informational materials

Advertising Coordinator, Utah Waterline, 1994-1999
- Prepared advertising artwork and copy
- Sold advertising space

Accountant, Dickinson & Associates, 1990-1994
- Collected data and prepared weekly, monthly, and yearly reports
- Prepared cost and profit reports, generated revision reports
- Communicated with banks and other financial institutions

Computer Support Specialist, Megawest, Inc., 1982-1990
- Provided instruction for clients in the use of accounting software
- Provided basic accounting instruction and training in the preparation of income statements and balance sheets
- Prepared reports with line specification and custom features
- Provided additional support for all software users

REFERENCES

Available when requested

SAM L. CHEN

1362 W. 11th • Amherst, MA 01002 • (413) 555-3889 • samchen@xxx.com

OBJECTIVE

Production department management in a progressive advertising firm.

SKILLS AND ATTRIBUTES

Publication
Familiar with entire publication process, from initial drafts to final distribution. Direct experience with planning, writing, editing, design, layout, and production of various documents and publications.

Computer/Desktop Publishing
Experienced with Macintosh-based desktop publishing systems, including graphic design, page layout software, and photo image setting techniques. Familiar with wide range of software on both Macintosh and Windows personal computer systems; exposure to use of UNIX-based systems.

Interpersonal Skills
Able to relate extremely well to others, comfortable in multicultural workplace, manage stress well. Experience and training in empathic listening, assertiveness, cultural awareness, interviewing, teaching, and group/interpersonal process.

EMPLOYMENT

Editor/Director, October 2000-present
Computer Engineering Network, College of Engineering
University of Massachusetts, Amherst, MA
Write, lay out, and assist in all aspects of producing the *CED Newsletter*, an award-winning monthly newsletter. Write and edit technical articles for the newsletter. Lay out and design various other publications, including brochures, technical documentation, and handbooks. Coordinate and schedule production.

EMPLOYMENT *(CONT.)*

Executive Director/Administrative Assistant, February 1998-October 2000
Neighborhood Housing Services, Easthampton, MA
Assessment and intake of clients for housing rehabilitation and purchase programs designed for low- and moderate-income persons. Managed revolving loan fund, including loan and credit counseling and servicing for high-risk loan profile. Created and designed homesteading program; obtained grants, contracts, and coordinated fund-raising for administration of all programs. Supervised construction and rehabilitation projects, public relations, and community organization efforts.

Assistant Manager/Sales Associate, December 1990-January 1998
Smith Brothers, Limited, Amherst, MA
Sales, customer relations, buying, and ordering.

EDUCATION

University of Massachusetts, Amherst, MA, Bachelor of Arts, December 1996
Honors Program, College of Literature, Science, and the Arts, 3.66 G.P.A.

College courses at other institutions: computer applications, real estate, property management.

RELATED EXPERIENCE

Served as member of various boards and committees for the City of Easthampton from 1998 to 2000, including the Community Relations Board (Secretary) and the Pesticide-Herbicide Advisory Committee.

Volunteer service to SOS Community Crisis Center in Springfield, MA, from 1995 to 1999, including phone and walk-in crisis work, on-call crisis team member, ongoing counselor, trainer, peer supervisor, and clinic program coordinator.

References Available Upon Request

JULIA D. MEIERSON

Route 1 Box 119 • Oakland, Maine 04963 • (207) 555-1103 • juliameierson@xxx.com

PRESENT EMPLOYMENT

The Square Café, Waterville, Maine   Since June 1998
Primary responsibilities include designing and buying advertisements in local media, coordinating schedule of advertising, and coordinating art gallery.

EDUCATION

Bates College, Lewiston, Maine   January 1993 to December 1996
Bachelor of Arts with High Honors in Anthropology and Religion
Honors Thesis: *Feminist Witchcraft: A Theological Analysis*

Activities:
Coordinator of Forum on Human Awareness, 1996
Coordinator of Women's Awareness, 1994

University of Jaffna, Jaffna, Sri Lanka   Fall semester, 1995
Conducted independent field study on maternity and child welfare.

University of Nottingham, Nottingham, England   Winter & Spring semesters, 1994
Conducted independent project at an abused women's shelter, working primarily with children of abused women.

The Evergreen State University, Olympia, Washington   Summer semester, 1993
Studied ecological agriculture at Olympia Fields Organic Farm.

WORK EXPERIENCE

Rape Crisis Assistance, Inc., Waterville, Maine   January 1998 to May 1998
Codirector. Coordinated volunteers and provided community education in Somerset County.

Family Planning, Skohegan and Waterville, Maine   January 1996 to January 1998
Family Planning Specialist. Provided reproductive health care and crisis counseling.

The *Harvard Post*, Harvard, Massachusetts   1996 to 1998
Reporter covering women's issues and activities in Harvard and Boston areas.

WRBC Radio, Bates College, Lewiston, Maine   1994 to 1995
WHMB Community Radio, Lewiston, Maine   1994 to 1995
Directed, produced, and announced weekly radio show of women's music.

***Bates Student*, Bates College, Lewiston, Maine   1993 to 1996**
Wrote biweekly opinion and events column for student newspaper.

REFERENCES ON REQUEST

—— TARA ANN BETHUNE ——

511 Northwest Second Avenue • Philadelphia, Pennsylvania 19104
(215) 555-8841 • Cell: (215) 555-1223
tarabethune@xxx.com

GOAL ——

To apply my skills and experience with advertising and marketing in a management position.

QUALIFICATIONS ——

- Marketing, advertising sales, graphic production.
- Records management, including accounts payable/receivable, payroll, inventory control, and tax reporting.
- Purchase of supplies to assure adequate inventories.
- Day-to-day management responsibilities, including scheduling, assigning activities, and program assessments.
- Computer literacy, experience with word processing computer applications.
- Public relations skills, including reception, sales, collections, and purchasing.
- Time management proficiency, promoting timely completion of projects and meeting deadlines.

EDUCATION ——

Community College of Philadelphia, Pennsylvania   **1999-present**

Business management courses with emphasis in retailing, advertising, marketing, accounting, and human relations. Also completed introductory computer courses.

Philadelphia College of Art, Pennsylvania   **1993-1999**

Associate of Arts Degree, Design Technology.

EXPERIENCE ——

Management Trainee. Regional School of Ballet, Philadelphia   **1997-1999**

Duties: Learned and implemented skills in daily management of dance school. Arranged advertising through local media sources. Planned development and marketing strategies. Completed billing report, payroll records, compiled accounts payable and receivable information. Collected unpaid balances. Ordered and maintained inventories. Supervised staff and scheduled work hours.

Camera Operator/Printer. Sir Speedy Printing, Philadelphia   **1995-1997**

Duties: Operated variety of camera and bindery equipment, including printer and platemaker. Assisted customers, completed sales transactions and reports, prepared advertising for local media and yellow pages. Began system of tracking advertising results to better determine advertising cost-effectiveness.

Printer. In and Out Printing, Philadelphia   **1993-1995**

Duties: Operated printing machine and darkroom equipment. Coordinated incoming work assignments. Performed pasteup, platemaking, and bindery duties. Trained newly hired employees. Composed, printed, and generated monthly newsletter. Carried out projects as assigned.

REFERENCES AVAILABLE ON REQUEST

Ian P. Robinson

1009 Selby Drive, Geneva, Illinois 60134
Home (630) 555-9984 • Work (630) 555-0228
ianrobinson@xxx.com

Objective

Advertising account manager with responsibility for developing and implementing advertising campaigns. Especially interested in opportunities that will take advantage of my verbal and written fluency in French.

Professional Experience

Genève Amerique, Geneva, IL. Manager and Buyer, 1999–current
- Develop, produce, and implement direct mail and newspaper advertising campaigns that have directly contributed to a 45% sales growth over four years.
- Buy and merchandise French textile and ceramic handcrafted items.
- Maintain financial control of $175,000 annual sales volume.
- Translate business-related documents, French-English/English-French.

Storefront Bookstore, Minneapolis, MN. Manager/Regional Planner, 1998–1999
- Responsible for effective visual presentation for three area stores.
- Trained and supervised ten employees.
- Controlled inventory and financial planning of $300,000 annual sales volume.

La France, Edina, MN. Counter Manager, 1995–1998
- Supervised staff of twelve waiters.
- Supervised food preparation and distribution.
- Integrated daily cash receipts into restaurant financial budget.

KMSR Radio, Collegeville, MN. Assistant Director of Programming, 1993–1995
News Announcer, DJ, 1991–1992
- Hired and scheduled staff of 75 volunteer disc jockeys.
- Implemented listener survey that increased funding by 63%.
- Wrote and engineered news programming and public service announcements.

Education

St. John's University, Collegeville, MN
Bachelor of Arts in Government and French, awarded 1998

Institute for American Universities, Aix-en-Provence, France
French language course work, 1996

University of Chicago, Chicago, IL
Specialized course work in photography, 2000
Specialized course work in desktop publishing and design, 1999

References available

jolene e. marks

3335 North Road
Bellevue, Colorado 80512
303-555-4886
jolenemarks@xxx.com

job sought

A position in advertising sales with a daily newspaper

education

Colorado State University, Fort Collins, CO
Bachelor of Arts in Journalism, June 2000
Concentration: News/Editorial

Valley College, Rockland, PA
Three semesters of liberal arts courses
Dean's List all semesters
Phi Theta Chi academic society

work history

Advertising Account Assistant, Bolling Publishing, Redondo Beach, CA   May-August 1996
Internship sponsored by Business Educational Foundation. Developed advertising base accounts, prepared sales presentations, closed sales, assisted with billing and record keeping.

Advertising Sales, *Movement Inc. Magazine*, Fort Collins, CO   1993-1996
Duties included ad sales, ad copywriting, producing pages via desktop publishing, fulfilling circulation, and maintaining relationships with advertisers and production department. Promoted from secretary to editor.

volunteer

Family Help Program, Rockland, PA 1990-1993
Worked one-on-one as "big sister" to young girls who had been physically or sexually abused.

Crisisline, Rockland, PA 1988-1990
Graduated from 70-hour training program. Volunteered as line worker. Fielded phone calls ranging from informative/referral to suicide prevention.

references

Available on request

■ RICHARD WALKER

2774 Tower Drive, Chicago, IL 60647   **(312) 555-8831**
richardwalker@xxx.com   **(312) 555-6655**

■ OBJECTIVE

To obtain a position that would both challenge and utilize my communication, desktop publishing, and graphic design talents.

■ EDUCATION

Illinois State University
Bachelor of Science Degree, December 1997
Major: Visual and Written Communication
Grade Point Average: 4.0 (major) / 3.5 (overall)

■ WORK EXPERIENCE

5/99 - Present   **RW Graphics, Chicago, IL**
Freelance Desktop Publisher/Designer. Involved in several freelance projects, including production editor and art director of *The College News*, a monthly independent publication; production of brochures and promotional packages for small businesses; and advertising creation, design, and production for small businesses.

10/97 - 5/99   ***Week's Worth* Magazine, Lake Zurich, IL.**
Editor and Designer. Started weekly arts, culture, and entertainment magazine, gaining a circulation base of 14,000 within fourteen months. Managed all aspects of marketing and promotion. Supervised advertising department staff for ad sales and self-promotion advertising campaigns. Managed all aspects of production. Assigned staff articles and edited freelance articles for publication. Designed magazine from cover to cover. Managed budget and payroll for 15-person staff.

6/96 - 10/97   ***Friday's* Magazine, *Daily Vidette*, Illinois State University, Normal, IL**
Editor. Assigned and edited staff stories. Created page layout and design. Wrote feature-length stories. Managed budget and eight-person staff for weekly entertainment magazine supplement to college newspaper.

page 1 of 2

■ WORK EXPERIENCE (CONT.)

2/96 - 10/97   **College of Arts and Sciences, Illinois State University, Normal, IL**
Newsletter Editor. Created eight-page newsletter using QuarkXPress. Interviewed faculty and student leaders. Wrote feature stories.

1/96 - 5/96   **Department of Communication, Illinois State University, Normal, IL**
Undergraduate Teaching Assistant, Community Relations Department. Assisted students in the creation, design, layout, and writing of a newsletter produced in PageMaker on the Macintosh.

8/95 - 5/96   ***Daily Vidette*, Illinois State University, Normal, IL**
Feature Writer and Columnist. Covered various entertainment events, wrote feature stories and weekly commentary column for Features department.

■ HONORS & AWARDS

Dean's List
General Assembly Scholar
Critical Film Review Award, Second Place, Illinois College Press Association
Public Relations Student Society of America

■ SPECIAL SKILLS

Thorough knowledge of desktop publishing and design programs, including QuarkXPress and Adobe PageMaker. Also have desktop graphics and writing experience using IBM and Macintosh software applications.

References and portfolio available upon request.

Drew Evan Carlisle

862 Main Street, Apt. 1
Durango, CO 81301
(303) 555-2261
Cell: (303) 555-9722
drewcarlisle@xxx.com

Job Objective: A career in the field of advertising

Experience: **Janus Advertising Agency, Boulder, Colorado**
Marketing and Sales Assistant, Summer 2001
• Assisted Marketing Manager in the areas of promotion, product development, and demographic research and analysis.

Telemarketing, Inc., Durango, Colorado
Telephone Sales, Summers 1999 and 2000

International House of Pancakes
Durango, Colorado
Waiter and Cashier, June 1997 to June 1999

Education: **Fort Lewis College, Durango, Colorado**
Bachelor of Arts in Communications, 2002
Major: Advertising. Major GPA: 4.0. Overall GPA: 3.75
• Dean's List each semester
• Business Club Treasurer
• Student Senate Representative for Communications Department
• Served on President's Commission for Student Equity

• Plan to pursue graduate studies toward a master's degree in advertising and marketing at Denver University, evening program.

Special Skills: • Fluent in Spanish
• Knowledge of Excel, MS Office, PageMaker, and Lotus SmartSuite
• Excellent communication skills

References: Available on request

Sujata T. Rao

sujatarao@xxx.com

26 East Three Penny Road • Detroit, Michigan 33290
(313) 555-2293 • FAX: (303) 555-2215

Career Objective

Art director for a large Midwest advertising agency.

Career Experience

Bernard Faruch Agency, Detroit, Michigan
Assistant Art Director, 1998 to present
Senior Staff Artist, 1996 to 1998
Staff Artist, 1994 to 1996

Directed creative teams assigned to advertising campaigns. Oversaw all artwork, design, production for print media advertisements. Hired artists, researchers, copywriters, and creative assistants. Conferred with clients and advertising sales managers to determine advertising strategy, market demographics, and positioning. Formulated design concepts. Assigned work to artists, writers, photographers, and production assistants.

Rao and Associates Design, Detroit, Michigan
President and Director, 1990 to 1994

Started graphic design business that attracted a wide variety of clients for production of advertisements for print media. Hired freelance graphic artists, photographers, and copywriters. Worked with clients to determine advertising strategy, audience, and medium. Developed advertising concepts. Prepared camera-ready mechanicals for advertisements, brochures, newsletters, annual reports, flyers, and inserts. Made sales presentations. Worked with various vendors for typesetting, camera work, prepress, and printing. Trained new employees in making sales presentations and developing advertising designs to fit a specific marketing strategy or audience.

Education

Museum School, Detroit, Michigan
Graphic Design Student, 1988 to 1990

Rhode Island School of Design, Providence, Rhode Island
Graphic Design Student, 1987 to 1988

Harvard University, Boston, Massachusetts
Bachelor of Arts in Advertising, 1987

References and portfolio are available on request.

SHANNON BARKER

226 Marquette #2 • Albuquerque, NM 87102
505/555-3119 • Cell: 505/555-2223 • shannonbarker@xxx.com

OBJECTIVE

A management position in advertising where I can utilize my marketing and management experience.

WORK EXPERIENCE

7-Eleven, Albuquerque, NM
Marketing Director, 1998-Present
Developed a successful marketing campaign for a convenience store chain. Implemented marketing strategies to increase sales by 23 percent at least-profitable outlets. Initiated and maintained positive working relationship with radio and print media representatives. Designed a training program for store managers and staff.

Arizona Register, **Phoenix, AZ**
Advertising Sales, 1994-1998
Sold space advertising to a variety of business and organizational clients. Maintained excellent communications with top clients. Made cold calls on businesses to encourage advertising. Responsible for 25 percent increase in regular advertiser base over four-year period. Coordinated with design and production departments to maintain quality in advertising products as client advocate.

Arizona Evening Herald, **Phoenix, AZ**
Classified Advertising Sales, 1993-1994
Sold classified advertising to private and business clients. Entered advertisements in computer system. Checked advertisements for accuracy. Billed clients for advertising. Made follow-up calls to increase run of advertising. Coordinated with advertising department on special issue discount offers in the classified section.

Other work experience includes advertising sales manager for student newspaper, University of Arizona; salesclerk for women's clothing boutiques; and sales representative for children's books sold door-to-door.

EDUCATION

University of Arizona, Phoenix, AZ
Bachelor of Science in Business, 1993. Major: Advertising and Marketing
Minor: Communications
Honors Project Award for Advertising Sales
Dean's List
Sigma Delta Gamma, Advertising Honorary

SEMINARS

Marketing Strategies in Advertising, 2000
Cooperative Advertising: Opportunities for the Next Century, 2000

REFERENCES

Portfolio and professional references will be furnished on request.

FREIDA M. CARTER

335 W. Fifth Street
Brooklyn, NY 12009
718/555-5375
freidacarter@xxx.com

ACADEMIC BACKGROUND

Brigham Young University
Provo, Utah
B.A. in Communications   April 2002
Minor: Advertising

SKILLS AND ACCOMPLISHMENTS

- Experienced with purchasing ad space in newspapers and magazines.
- Developed concepts for advertising campaign.
- Improved profitability by switching ads from publications that produced marginal results to significantly more productive ones.
- Directed and implemented readership survey.
- Incorporated analysis from readership survey into market study for presentation to potential advertisers.
- Experienced with advertising sales, billing, rates, and customer relations.

WORK EXPERIENCE

Managing Editor, *The Daily Universe*, Brigham Young Student Newspaper, Provo, UT
January 1998 to April 2002

Advertising Intern, Brooklyn Savings Bank, Brooklyn, NY
Summer 1999

Shift Manager, Rocky Mountain Drive-In, Provo, UT
May 1998 to November 2001

REFERENCES

Available on request.

Margaret Lawrence

334-555-3322 • margaretlawrence@xxx.com

Present Address
2524 Tulsa Hwy.
Tulsa, Oklahoma 74115

Permanent Address
299 Starker Dr.
Montgomery, Alabama 36117

Objective
To obtain an entry-level position in advertising copywriting.

Education
University of Tulsa, Oklahoma
Expected graduation date, August 2003
Degree: B.A. in Advertising, double minor in Journalism and Marketing

Work Experience
PhotoSource, Tulsa, Oklahoma
(part-time, August 1999 to present)
Advertising space sales • Copywriting • Order-handling
Billing • Customer relations

The Montgomery Advertiser, Montgomery, Alabama
(June 1998 to September 1999)
Special studies intern • Design and layout of advertisements
Classified ad sales • Ad copywriting

Related Course Work
Advertising Strategy
Advertising Copywriting
Advertising Design
Advertising Campaign Management
Public Relations Writing and Research
Electronic Design and Production
Marketing for Communication
Broadcast Newswriting

Activities
Sigma Delta Chi Honorary Society (Journalism)
Advertising Club
Pi Kappa Phi, national sorority
Softball team

References available on request, along with portfolio

THERESA VASQUEZ

33528 Santa Monica Boulevard
Los Angeles, California 90088
(213) 555-8842 (days)
(213) 555-3331 (evenings)
theresavasquez@xxx.com

CAREER OBJECTIVE

Traffic manager at an advertising agency or in a corporate
advertising department.

WORK EXPERIENCE

CONNECTIONS MAGAZINE, HOLLYWOOD, CALIFORNIA
ASSISTANT PRODUCTION MANAGER, 1998 TO PRESENT

Oversee all aspects of production and printing at a national
publication. Involved in extensive client and advertising agency
contact. Coordinate with editorial and advertising department heads
for positioning of advertising. Work with graphic designers on
production specifications and proofing. Handle in-depth contact
with other media and service vendors. Produce copy and
mechanicals for advertisements.

HAVENER'S, BURBANK, CALIFORNIA
ASSISTANT TO PROMOTION DIRECTOR, 1994 TO 1998

Conducted all in-store promotions and coordinated special events
for large department store. Placed advertising and publicity notices
in local media. Prepared advertising copy and designed mock-ups
for promotional ads. Wrote text for radio and television spot
announcements. Consulted on grand opening of Hollywood store.
Provided customer assistance.

BRUINLIFE, UCLA STUDENT YEARBOOK
LOS ANGELES, CALIFORNIA
ADVERTISING MANAGER, 1993 TO 1994

Directed advertising sales for 45-page advertising section of student yearbook. Developed sales strategies, assigned territories to sales staff, conducted weekly sales report meetings, tracked sales and billing. Coordinated advertising design and production with graphic design staff. Prepared mock-up ads for sales samples to encourage ad sales for target clients. Developed special ad pages for student advertisements and directed sales efforts.

EDUCATION

University of California, Los Angeles
B.S. degree in Advertising and Marketing, 1994

HONORS

1992	Cum Laude
1992–1994	Dean's List
1991–1994	Wilma Morris Scholarship
1994–present	Member, National Association of Student Advertisers
1994	UCLA Advertising Sales Award
1994	UCLA Best Advertising Designer

REFERENCES

Available on request.

ANTHONY J. MAREK

2274 Swanson Place • Hartford, Connecticut 06112 • (203) 555.2176

OBJECTIVE

To obtain a position as Art Director.

EXPERIENCE

Creative Advertising Designs, Inc./Hartford   **2000-present**
Senior Art Director, Production Manager, Account Executive

Small advertising/typesetting studio. Responsible for overseeing all projects. Handle all daily business. Supervise three typesetters and four artist/designers. Projects include print media space advertisements, catalogs, point-of-purchase, direct mail, consumer, business to business, and recruitment advertising with a wide variety of accounts.

Patterson & Associates, Marketing & Advertising Agency/New Haven   **1998-2000**
Senior Art Director

Managed three-person art department. Supervised layout, design, illustration, and production of consumer, recruitment, and automotive accounts.

Sears Corporation, Corporate Advertising Department/Chicago   **1993-1998**
Senior Artist, Staff Artist, Production Assistant

Responsibilities included layout, design, illustration, storyboards, and production for corporate clients, including newspaper advertising department, automotive dealership, financial organizations, and advertising agencies.

EDUCATION & TRAINING

Art Institute of Chicago
Bachelor of Fine Arts Degree, Graphic Design & Illustration, 1992

How to Buy Printing/Hartford
Two-week seminar on printing specifications, purchasing, and related services.

American Association of Graphic Artists/National
Attended seminars as part of national and regional conventions in areas of electronic prepress, magazine advertising design, media choices for advertisers, among others.

AWARDS

Danny Award, Best Automotive Ad/Client, Connecticut Buick Dealers' Association
Art Institute of Chicago, Design Annual, Honorable Mention

MEMBERSHIPS

Graphic Design Consortium/Hartford
American Association of Graphic Artists/National

References are available on request.

Mallory Aiken

7300 N. Washburn
Trenton, NJ 08690

malloryaiken@xxx.com
201-555-1246 (days)
201-555-0193 (evenings)

Career Objective

To gain an entry-level design position where my creative skills
in design and illustration can be best utilized.

Education

Bachelor of Fine Arts, May 2002
Southern Illinois University, Carbondale, IL
Major: Design
Concentration: Visual Communication
G.P.A. 4.0 in art; 3.4 overall

Career-Related Skills

Worked with IBM Publisher's Paintbrush
Experienced with Macintosh desktop publishing, PageMaker
Creative and technical drawing skills
Strong illustration capabilities (pastel, charcoal, airbrush)
Knowledge of Russian and Japanese

Work Experience

Micro Media, Trenton, NJ
Reception/Customer Service/Data Entry
Summers 1998-2001

Jimmy John's Gourmet Sub Shop, Carbondale, IL
Waitress/Sandwich Creator/Cashier
1996-1998

Osco Drugs, Trenton, NJ
Cashier/Stock Person
1993-1996

Kelley Services, Trenton, NJ
Office/Clerical Work
1991-1992

References

Furnished on request

William L. Finchley Jr.

11249 Madison Way • Shreveport, Louisiana 71101 • (318) 555-2485
williamfinchley@xxx.com

Career Objective
To obtain a position as art director for an advertising agency where my skills in design and strategic planning may be effectively utilized.

Skills Summary
- Extensive experience in the greeting card industry.
- Key positions include Art Director, Assistant Art Director, Line Planner, and Designer.
- Excellent communication, supervisory, and creative skills.

Professional Experience
Heri Fayette, Inc., Shreveport, LA   *3/96 - Present*
Art Director
- Hold complete responsibility for Christmas and special All Occasion cards, stationery, and gift lines.
- Participate in corporate strategic planning.
- Plan and balance designs in subject matter and price. Choose paper, operations, and trims.
- Direct staff and work with freelancers.
- Provide press approvals and direct activity of graphic department.
- Revise old dies for new design appearance.
- Design new cards, prepare finished working drawings, die drawings, and cutting samples.
- Choose sentiments, envelopes, and presentation of completed design on mount.

Package Source Inc., Eureka Division, Shreveport, LA   *7/93 - 2/96*
Planner and Designer
- Planned and designed package trims and gift tags.
- Designed and completed finished art for packaging of tins.

Greetings, Inc., Shreveport, LA   *3/87 - 7/93*
Head Designer
- Color separator for greeting cards.
- Head designer and line planner for Christmas, all other seasonal lines, and a complete everyday line of greeting cards.
- Coordinated art department projects as assistant to the art director.
- Coordinated all projects with advertising department for promotion of special card lines.

Art Education
McNeese State University, Lake Charles, LA
Associate Degree in Design and Illustration, 1987

References on Request

JAMES ANDREW NOVIKYA

3352 Sander Drive • Apartment 23 • Pittsburgh, PA 28901
412.555.7450 • jamesnovikya@xxx.com

EXPERIENCE

5/99 - present

Design Engineer, Palatine Corporation, Pittsburgh, PA
Design and develop product display concepts and illustrate renderings, coordinate computer graphic design orders for client jobs, and oversee inventory control and product distribution.

6/97 - present

Designer, Self-Employed
Developed concepts and carried them to camera-ready state, production, or actual print. Examples of graphic works include book covers, program layout. Also furniture design and interior design consultation. Established clientele and maintained customer service.

3/97 - 5/99

Gallery Support Staff, Houston Sutton Galleries Pittsburgh, PA
Responsible for handling and maintaining works of art before and after sale, upkeep of physical plant, and repairs to artworks.

5/95 - 1/97

Manager, Stouffer Street Bar and Grill Philadelphia, PA
Responsible for banking, scheduling security, customer service, and payroll.

EDUCATION

5/97

Bachelor of Arts, Arts Administration
Andrews University, Berrien Springs, MI

1/98

Studies in Architectural Design
Albright College, Reading, PA

AFFILIATIONS

2/97 - present   Member, Progressive Design Group of Pennsylvania
9/94 - present   Alpha Lambda Arts Fraternity

References and Portfolio Available

Stuart G. Swanson

1644 Howard Street   Pontiac, MI 48057   616/555-1197
stuartswanson@xxx.com

OBJECTIVE   To join the advertising and promotion department of a large arts organization where my skills in arts marketing and graphic design may be directed toward advertising and fund-raising projects.

EDUCATION   **Master of Arts Administration, December 1999**
Sangamon State University, Springfield, IL
G.P.A. 3.9
Relevant Courses

Arts Administration	Organizational Dynamics
Marketing	Museum Management
Fund-raising	Financial Management
Public Policy	Business Law

Bachelor of Science, Art, May 1998
University of Wisconsin, Madison, WI
G.P.A. 3.4; Dean's List, 1997-1998
Relevant Courses

Painting	Drawing
Printmaking	Graphic Design
Typography	Computer Art

EXPERIENCE
1999   **Michigan Arts Board, Percent for Art Program, Pontiac, MI**
Program Assistant
■ Designed flyers, posters, and advertisements announcing competitions
■ Served as administrative assistant to public art program coordinator
■ Researched other public art programs for policy development purposes
■ Prepared detailed reports on the program's operational effectiveness
■ Systemized slide registry and program files
■ Assisted in art and artist selection procedures

1996-1997   **Michigan Art-in-Architecture Program, Detroit, MI**
Intern
■ Served as an intern for the public art program
■ Designed and produced a collection brochure
■ Wrote text for brochures and catalog
■ Assembled slide presentations and updated project files
■ Assisted in selection committee meetings

References on request

––– Yuri T. Lobojko –––

2245 South Lawn • Los Angeles, California 90016
(213) 555-9197 (Day) • (213) 555-2983 (Evening) • yurilobojko@xxx.com

Career Objective ––

Advertising Director for a television station.

Skills and Achievements ––

Promotion and Marketing

- Wrote and designed advertisements of various lengths and short promotional spots
- Evaluated content and direction of station promotions
- Handled market research/demographic studies
- Consulted station managers and executives on marketing strategies

Video Production and Editing

- Supervised shooting procedures, audio, lighting, casting, and editing
- Wrote and edited scripts for advertisements and two 30-minute public service documentaries
- Determined production values for marketing accounts
- Oversaw postproduction and placement
- Coordinated presentations to clients

Media Planning and Management

- Advised clients on media strategies
- Oversaw media budgets
- Supervised design teams
- Negotiated spot rates for clients

Related Employment ––

Trumball Advertising, Hollywood, California
Media Planner, 1994 - Present

Starnes and Starnes, Inc., San Diego, California
Assistant Media Buyer, 1990 - 1994

KQRY Radio FM, San Francisco, California
Advertising Assistant, 1988 - 1990

Education ––

University of Southern California, Los Angeles
Bachelor of Arts in Business; Minor in Film/Video Production
Degree awarded June 1988
Graduated cum laude
Awarded second place in USC Filmmakers Annual, 1986; honorable mention, 1988

Christine Westerberg

222 Joslyn Street, N.W.
Seattle, Washington 98102
(206) 555-1223
christinewesterberg@xxx.com

Objective   To obtain a position as an assistant advertising executive

Achievements
~ Coordinated media planning and buying
~ Researched potential markets for ad campaigns
~ Supervised artwork, layout, and production
~ Handled sales promotions
~ Supervised trade shows and press shows
~ Arranged and conducted sales meetings and presentations
~ Designed and distributed press packets
~ Developed marketing strategies
~ Planned marketing and advertising campaigns
~ Wrote and distributed press releases
~ Served as liaison between clients and media representatives
~ Acted as liaison to outside advertising agencies

Work Experience
Advertising Coordinator, 2000 – present
RHB Furniture Design Center, Seattle

Assistant Coordinator of Advertising, 1996 – 2000
Nordstrom, Central Office, Seattle

Assistant Sales Manager, 1994 – 1996
Nordstrom, Bellevue

Salesperson, 1992 – 1994
Nordstrom, Bellevue

Education
Bachelor of Arts, English
University of Washington, 1992

Seminars
"Mail Order and Direct Mail Advertising"
University of Washington Business Center

"Account Management"
Seattle University Summer Program

References   Available on request

Trevor Ghering

323 South Whilelaw • Atlanta, Georgia 30316
404/555-8846 • trevorghering@xxx.com

Designer/Illustrator   **Atlanta, GA**   **1992 to present**
Operate freelance business interacting directly with publishers, agencies, manufacturers, distributors, film and slide producers, and entrepreneurs.

Client Contact   As consulting art director, confer with clients to interpret the design problem and involve them on design approaches. Establish budget perimeters. Determine illustrative needs. Advise on reproduction needs.

Creativity   Conceptualize design solution. Produce layouts translating clients' information into display form. Select typography, color, illustrations, photography, and other imaging.

Production   Supervise typesetting, photography, or other specialized art as needed. Produce finished keyline art for reproduction. Coordinate with printers and other service bureaus for production of finished product.

Experience   Produce work for print and film advertisements, brochure literature, books, publications, catalogs, posters, logos, trademarks, annual reports, labels and packages, slide programs, animated sequences, and games.

Illustration   Produce illustration for projects with both traditional methods and computerized graphics software. Products illustrated include educational, technical, symbolic, humorous, whimsical, and traditional.

Education   Bachelor of Fine Arts, Graphic Design
California College of Art and Crafts, Oakland, CA
Degree awarded 1992

References and portfolio available on request.

Gil Sanders

221 West Ventura Boulevard   818/555-7452
Santa Monica, California 90403   gilsanders@xxx.com

Career Objective   Traffic manager for an advertising agency that will utilize
my creativity, organization, and communication skills.

Experience
- Oversaw all aspects of production and printing at a national publication
- Actively involved in client and agency communications
- Organized all art, mechanicals, and final films with stripping department
- Handled in-depth media background contact with other media
- Conducted all in-store promotions and events for the state's largest bookstore
- Produced copy for ads
- Placed advertising and publicity in local publications
- Worked as operations director for small mail-order company

Work History   *Broad Horizons* **Magazine, Santa Monica, California**
Assistant to the Production Manager, 2001 - Present

**Radio Shack, Inc., Corporate Headquarters
San Francisco, California**
Assistant to the Promotion/Advertising Director,
1998 - 2001

Education   Bachelor of Arts, Business Administration, 1998
Minor: Advertising
University of California at Santa Cruz

Seminar: "Time and Resources Management" 1998
Workshop: "Production and Printing Innovations" 2000

Honors   Reedmore Scholarship, 1996 - 1998
Dean's List, 1996 - 1998
Best Undergraduate Project, UCSC Honors College

References   Available on request

PARKER ALLEN

334 Market Avenue   St. Louis, MO 53190
315-555-2468   parkerallen@xxx.com

OBJECTIVE

A career in media services where I can utilize my skills in marketing, organization, and communication.

EDUCATION

University of Missouri, Kansas City. Degree awarded June 2003
B.A. in Advertising
Major field G.P.A.: 3.75
Overall G.P.A.: 3.45

Honors & Activities
Honors College graduate
Business Representative to Associated Student Government
Chair, Honors Curriculum Student Committee
Student Representative, College of Business Promotion and Tenure Committee
Officer, African-American Students Cultural Association

WORK EXPERIENCE

Markham Advertising, Kansas City, MO
Advertising Intern, Summer 2002

Worked with advertising account executive and marketing manager in the areas of promotion, product development, market research, and demographic analysis. Through research and market analysis, identified prime prospects for target advertising. Coordinated production of a series of target advertisements directed at college students for a client who operated a local recreation organization. Received highest possible rating for internship.

Big River Marketing, Kansas City, MO
Telemarketing salesperson, 1999 - 2003

Missouri Highway Department, St. Louis, MO
Flagger/Driver, Road Construction Crew, Summers 1996 - 1999

REFERENCES AVAILABLE AS REQUESTED

Wendy Miller
wendymiller@xxx.com

Present Address
122 Ketchum Hwy
Auburn, Alabama 36830
(205) 555-2485

Permanent Address
554 Tremblay Drive
Montgomery, Alabama 36117
(334) 555-3335

OBJECTIVE   Obtain an entry-level position in advertising

EDUCATION   Auburn University, Auburn, Alabama
Expected date of graduation, August 2003
Degree: Bachelor of Arts
Major: Advertising with a double minor in Public Relations and
    Marketing

WORK HISTORY   **Village Photographers, Auburn, Alabama (9/00 to present)**
Representative to organizations at Auburn University, Auburn
University at Montgomery, Lagrange College, Huntingdon College, and Troy State University. Responsibilities include order-handling, customer relations, and preparation of company newsletters.

**The Montgomery Advertiser, Montgomery, Alabama
(6/99 to 9/00)**
Special studies intern: responsibilities included design and layout of advertisements and ad pages on Harris pagination system, copyediting, and research.

COURSE WORK

Advertising Case Studies	Advertising Campaign
Advertising Writing	Market Research
Survey of Research Methods	Photojournalism
Electronic Field Production	Marketing for Communication
Broadcast Newswriting	Feature Writing
Newswriting	

ACTIVITIES   Sigma Delta Chi journalism honorary
Advertising Club
WEGL-911 FM news announcer
Student yearbook news writer and copyeditor
Pi Beta Phi national sorority

REFERENCES   Available

JEFFREY SCOTT WINSTON JR.

22 Melrose Park Lane   jeffreywinston@xxx.com
Savannah, Georgia 30290   (912) 555-3324

EDUCATION

Savannah University, Savannah, Georgia   **M.S. in Communications, 2003**

Relevant course work: advertising in print media, advertising in radio, advertising in television, public relations, ad copywriting, marketing research methods, strategic methods in advertising and public relations, management, behavioral communications, statistical methods.

Research project: Advertising sales strategies and results in five urban and five rural radio stations, controlled for staff and budget resources.

University of Nevada, Las Vegas   **B.S. in Journalism, 2001**

Relevant course work: ad copywriting, public relations, communications media, reporting, history of advertising and the media, storyboarding, visual presentation strategies.

EXPERIENCE

Sophronia Digest, **Savannah, Georgia**   **Summer Advertising Intern, 2002**

Served in advertising sales. Wrote sales letter to established and potential clients, notifying them of special issues and deadline dates. Received and cataloged camera-ready ads for placement in magazine. Worked with advertising design department to develop concepts and copy for self-promotion advertisements. Assisted with office management and billing.

University of Nevada, Las Vegas   **Research/Office Assistant, 1999-2001**

Served School of Journalism as research assistant and office assistant. Worked with faculty on media research projects. Assisted with data entry, statistical analysis, and documentation. Assisted with editing of quarterly alumni newsletter. Prepared and sent bulk mailings. Gained experience with IBM and Macintosh desktop publishing and communications software and statistical analysis software used in media research.

HONORS & ACTIVITIES

Journalism Honorary, Sigma Delta Chi
Advertising Association, Secretary, 1999-2001
Marshfield Scholarship for Journalism
Dean's List, 1999-2001

REFERENCES AVAILABLE ON REQUEST

Franklin Jordan Andrews

66 Traver Lane • Lincoln, Nebraska 68508
402/555-1967 • Cell: 402/555-3375
franklinandrews@xxx.com

Job Objective

Position as Advertising Manager for large national corporation. Willing to relocate.

Employment History

Director of Operations, *Outdoor Life Magazine*, Lincoln, NE, 2000 - Present
▼ Supervise 22 regional managers and office with 385 employees. Oversee all central office operations, including circulation, advertising sales, promotion and marketing, and $25 million budget administration. Developed and supervise new advertising sales management team, which produced a 20% increase in ad sales revenue over two years.

Assistant to General Manager, *Outdoor Life Magazine*, Lincoln, NE, 1998 - 2000
▼ Coordinated all of the magazine's configuration changes. Served as operations liaison to the European edition of *Outdoor Life*. Initiated subscription sales programs and formulated marketing strategies. Increased sales of subscription mailing lists through target advertising campaign. Developed and implemented several edition modifications to boost circulation sales and optimize advertising revenue.

Advertising Manager, *Sunset Magazine*, Menlo Park, CA 1992 - 1998
▼ Directed operations of five regional offices, with a sales staff of 84 and 35 support staff. Served as liaison with general management. Developed new advertising sections in order to target ad sales. Boosted advertising revenue base by $7.5 million over three years.

Regional Sales Manager, *Sunset Magazine*, Seattle, WA 1990 - 1992
▼ Met with corporate advertising representative to coordinate strategy and make sales presentations. Worked closely with corporate advertisers to plan space acquisition and optimal presentations.

Page 1 of 2

Employment History (cont.)

Advertising Sales Representative, *Sunset Magazine*, Seattle, WA 1987 - 1990
▼ Handled six major national corporate accounts. Coordinated advertising sales team in regional office. Developed sales presentations for special advertising sections. Brought in several new corporate clients over two-and-a-half-year period.

Media Buyer, Julian Friedan Advertising Agency, Boston, MA 1984 - 1987
▼ Served as media liaison between corporate clients and media sales representatives. Purchased space advertising in newspapers, magazines, radio, and television, including cable and network TV. Devised timetables and strategies in conjunction with media research and market analysis reports. Negotiated ad rates for corporate clients.

Media Researcher, *World Magazine*, Amherst, MA, 1980 - 1984
▼ Tracked market changes, with responsibility for preparing reports on significant developments and potential for impacts on advertising sales. Worked with advertising sales department on developing demographic data.

Education

M.B.A., University of Washington, Seattle, WA, 1987
B.S., University of Massachusetts, Amherst, MA, 1980

Professional Memberships

National Association of Magazine Publishers
International Association of Business Communicators
International Advertisers Association

References are provided upon request.

TERRANCE BULIEGH

613 Vineview Road, Providence, RI 02154   **Telephone (401) 555-6978**
terrancebuliegh@xxx.com   **Cell (401) 555-8332**

JOB OBJECTIVE
A management position in cable television advertising sales where my skills in planning, strategy, and sales can be utilized to increase sales revenue.

RELEVANT EXPERIENCE
- Sold space in television for four major clients for the automotive industry.
- Served as liaison between clients and television and radio salespeople.
- Bought local television and radio advertising space for large retail department store.
- Sold space for daytime programming on local television station.
- Advised station manager on content and suitability of advertisements and potential liability.
- Worked with creative departments to develop advertisement concepts for potential clients.

WORK HISTORY
AdMedia Agency, Providence, RI
Space Sales, Broadcast Media Division
October 1999 to present

WVIR Television, Bangor, ME
Television Space Sales
June 1996 to September 1999

KQRX Radio FM, Eugene, OR
Staff Sales Assistant, Advertising Department
June 1994 to April 1996

EDUCATION
Broadcast Media B.A. 1994
Oregon State University, Corvallis, OR

Honors
Best Senior Project, Broadcast Media Communications Department, 1994
Dean's List, 1992 to 1994
Rijken Junior Scholarship in Broadcast Media, 1992 to 1993

References provided upon request.

Samuel J. Barstow

132 S. Pennsylvania Ave.
Washington, D.C. 02165
202-555-3364
samuelbarstow@xxx.com

Objective

A career in advertising.

Work History

On Broadway Magazine, New York, NY
Assistant Production Manager, 2000 - Present

Oversee all aspects of production and printing at the central office. Work closely with advertising sales clients on advertising placement and scheduling. Organize all art, mechanicals, and final film with art department. Produce copy for ads.

Market Start, Washington, D.C.
Assistant to Production Manager, 1996 - 2000

Worked with promotion director to plan in-store promotion and events. Coordinated all activities in preparation for events. Purchased advertising space to promote events and special promotions. Worked with graphic designers to develop banners, flyers, and advertisements. Wrote advertising copy. Scheduled special celebrity guests and made arrangements for their travel and hospitality.

Education

Georgetown University, Washington, D.C.
B.S. in Communications, 1996

Relevant course work: advertising, promotions and public relations, advertising copywriting, public relations writing, marketing and sales, strategic planning.

Activities: Business and Advertising Society, Chair of Campus Cultural Diversity Task Force, Chamber Music Ensemble, Georgetown University Symphony Orchestra.

References

Available on request.

Aleisha Clarke

445 S. Magnolia
Baton Rouge, LA 20928
504/555-4485
504/555-2469
aleishaclarke@xxx.com

Career Objective

Advertising sales assistant position where I can effectively utilize my background in advertising, marketing, and sales.

Education

University of Louisiana, Baton Rouge
Bachelor of Arts, Advertising 2003

Major Fields: Advertising, Marketing, Public Relations, Business Management

Honors

Summa Cum Laude, 2003
Dean's List
Advertising Senior Award for Best Ad Campaign
International Newspaper Advertising and Marketing Executives First Award
Honors in Advertising, American Advertising Federation, National Student Advertising Contest

Work Experience

Rouge et Noire, Inc., Baton Rouge, LA
Advertising Intern, Summer 2002
  Handled three accounts of advertising agency. Worked with designers to develop ad concepts and designs. Wrote ad copy. Assisted with traffic control. Met with clients to discuss strategy and target markets. Served as intermediary between client and account executives.

University of Louisiana, Baton Rouge, LA
Advertising Manager, Yearbook Staff, 2002 – 2003
  Supervised advertising sales staff for yearbook. Coordinated sales of 22 pages of advertising. Met with corporate and individual clients to make sales presentations. Worked with design staff to develop advertisements. Wrote ad copy. Assisted with production of final ads. Distributed proof copies for review and approval from clients. Provided informational assistance to clients and yearbook manager. Exceeded budget projections for advertising sales revenue.

References

Provided upon request

JAMILLA STEWART-LAWRENCE

jamillastewart@xxx.com

Present Address
125 W. Hollis Ave., No. 6
Charlotte, NC 28230
(704) 555-2789

Permanent Address
556 E. Marquette St.
Richmond, VA 18975
(804) 555-2112

JOB OBJECTIVE: To obtain a challenging position in the field of advertising.

EDUCATION: Bachelor of Arts, Broadcast Journalism and Advertising
June 2002, University of North Carolina, Charlotte
Minor: Psychology

EXPERIENCE: **Advertising/Public Relations Intern**
University Savings Bank, Charlotte, North Carolina
April to June, 2002
Developed and implemented promotional ideas. Created, designed, and composed advertising copy and graphics on desktop publishing systems. Served as assistant editor of employee newsletter.

Advertising Campaign
Advanced Advertising Project, University of North Carolina, Charlotte
Fall 2001
Assisted in the creation of a new Perrier campaign designed to position the product against the diet soft-drink industry. Campaign selected by Perrier Corporation for implementation.

Resident Advisor
University of North Carolina, Charlotte
September to June, 1998 to 2000
Developed and ran more than 20 programs dealing with current issues in education, culture, religion, and health. Selected to edit campus residence hall newsletter.

Television/Radio Intern
WIRO-TV, WIRE News Radio, Richmond, Virginia
Summer 1999
Independently wrote more than 50 advertisement spots and public service announcements, working with clients. Updated advertising prospects file. Worked with advertising sales crew to develop sales strategies.

ACHIEVEMENTS: Outstanding Performance Award, University Savings Bank
Alumni Relations Chairperson, Gamma Phi Beta Sorority
Executive Council Member, Gamma Phi Beta

References provided on request

Reece Hartshore

1986 21st Avenue S.E.
Manhattan, KS 66502
(316) 555-8552
reecehartshore@xxx.com

Professional Goal

To obtain an entry-level position with a dynamic advertising agency.

Experience

- Developed and implemented promotional ideas.
- Assisted with development of national advertising campaign.
- Work with strategy team to develop new product position.
- Created, designed, and composed advertising copy and graphics.
- Trained on desktop publishing and computer graphics software.
- Made advertising sales calls to prospective radio advertising clients.
- Wrote advertising copy for radio commercial spots.
- Worked with advertising sales department to increase client base.
- Wrote and edited company newsletter.
- Received outstanding performance award for distinguished work.
- Served as alumni relations coordinator for national fraternity.
- Developed and promoted educational and cultural programs.

Education

Bachelor of Science, Business, 1998
Duke University, Durham, NC

Work History

WROC-FM Radio, Manhattan, KS, 1/98 to present
Advertising Sales Associate

Bank of North Carolina, Durham, NC, 7/96 to 1/98
Assistant to the Vice President for Advertising and Promotion

References are available on request.

JORGE ALCALA

224 E. 14th Street
Cincinnati, OH 45202

513/555-2896
513/555-9824
jorgealcala@xxx.com

JOB OBJECTIVE

Media planning position with an advertising agency

SKILLS AND ACHIEVEMENTS

MEDIA PLANNING

- Headed strategic planning team that handled twelve major corporate accounts
- Advised clients on media strategies
- Consulted with clients on marketing goals and helped translate into specific, action-oriented plans
- Oversaw media budgets and authorized space advertising purchases
- Determined and implemented marketing objectives
- Consulted with corporate clients on market segment and demographics research analysis
- Negotiated spot rates and frequency discounts for corporate clients

PROMOTION AND MARKETING

- Wrote and designed promotion pieces for distribution to media
- Evaluated intended direction of promotional campaigns
- Handled market research, demographic research, and analysis
- Made sales presentations to clients

EMPLOYMENT HISTORY

Sarton Advertising, Inc., Cincinnati, OH
Associate Media Planner, 1999 - present

Graves and Abright, Ltd., Cleveland, OH
Assistant Media Buyer, 1996 - 1999

Macy's, Chicago, IL
Advertising Assistant, 1994 - 1996

EDUCATION

Capital University, Columbus, OH
B.A. in Economics, 1994, with a minor in Advertising

REFERENCES AVAILABLE

DUNCAN STUART McPHERSON

3359 Potter Avenue East • Boston, MA 02115
602/555-2956 • duncanmcpherson@xxx.com

JOB OBJECTIVE

Advertising copywriting position

EDUCATION

Bachelor of Arts, Journalism and Advertising
March 2001, University of Massachusetts
Minor: Public Relations Writing

EMPLOYMENT AND RELEVANT EXPERIENCE

ADVERTISING/PUBLIC RELATIONS WRITING

Editor and Writer for employee newsletter, *Banknotes*
Massachusetts First Bank, Boston
April 2001 to present
Develop and coordinate promotional events and campaigns. Create, design, and write ad copy for institutional ads. Produce ads on desktop publishing software using IBM PC.

Intern, Advertising and Marketing Department
Crystal Springs, Boston
Summer 2000
Developed marketing strategy and complete print media ad campaign for local bottled water company as part of a class project. Campaign was adapted for use in four eastern sales regions.

PROMOTIONS

Student Activities Bureau, Assistant Programmer
University of Massachusetts, Boston
1996 to 2000
Developed and promoted speakers' forum and group discussions on wide variety of current events and topics. Scheduled presentations by community leaders. Handled all publicity for events.

NEWSWRITING

Intern, News Department
WBMG Radio News
Summer 1998
Independently wrote over 50 broadcast news stories. Updated and revised reporters' stories. Developed skills in interviewing and research techniques. Assisted with writing of advertising spots and public service announcements. Exercised editorial judgment in story selection and order of presentation during news segment.

ACHIEVEMENTS AND MEMBERSHIPS

Dean's List, University of Massachusetts
Merit Award, Spot News Story, BYBA Annual 1999
Boston Young Broadcasters Association
Sigma Delta Chi, Journalism Society
Massachusetts Writers' Collective

References are available on request.

DAMONE X. WILSON

3340 W. Moreno St., Apt. 17
Rutland, VT 05701
(802) 555-2948
damonewilson@xxx.com

JOB SOUGHT: Management position in the advertising department of a major food manufacturing company.

RELEVANT EXPERIENCE:

Management
- Managed sales/marketing staff that included advertising account managers and sales representatives.
- Monitored and studied the effectiveness of a national distribution and marketing network.
- Oversaw all aspects of sales and marketing budgets.

Advertising
- Represented company to advertising agencies and retailers in order to develop advertising strategies for new products.
- Organized and planned convention displays and strategies.
- Designed and executed direct-mail advertising campaign that identified market needs and new options for products.

Development
- Conceived ads, posters, and displays for point-of-purchase sales in department stores and grocery store chains.
- Initiated and published monthly newsletter that was distributed to current and potential retailers.

EMPLOYMENT HISTORY: Maple Confections, Rutland, VA
National Sales Manager, 1999 - present
Account Manager, 1997 - 1999
Assistant Account Manager, 1996 - 1997
Sales Assistant, 1994 - 1996

EDUCATION: B.A. in English, 1994
Northwestern University, Evanston, IL

REFERENCES: Available

Angela Fuentes

2120 Market, Apt. 14
Dallas, Texas 73389
206-555-2004
angelafuentes@xxx.com

Career Objective

Advertising assistant position where I can utilize my skills in organization, planning, and writing.

Employment History

Dallas Senior Center, Dallas, TX
Administrative Assistant to Director of Public Relations, 2000 to Present
Write and distribute news releases about Center events, educational programs, and issues. Maintain personal media contacts. Prepare and edit copy for advertisements, brochures, posters, and public service radio announcements. Develop advertising schedule and negotiate space rates and frequency discounts for print and radio advertising. Coordinate special events programming and implement plans. Handle all booking for live entertainment. Prepare and distribute newsletter to patrons.

Center for Personal Growth, Dallas, TX
Office Manager, 1996 to 2000
Coordinated workshops and seminars for continuing education program. Taught workshop on obtaining free publicity for local events. Supervised an office staff of eight. Coordinated all travel and hospitality arrangements for visiting dignitaries. Maintained business calendar. Organized staff meetings. Made all arrangements for national convention. Prepared financial reports. Handled payroll and supervised bookkeeping and budgeting functions.

Education

Dallas Christian College, Dallas, TX, 1995
B.A. in English with minor in Psychology

Special Skills

Typing, 75 wpm; dictation; bookkeeping; word processing; computer graphics

References provided on request.

HAN SO WAN
Illustration • Photography • Design • Production

200 Wimmer Blvd. • La Jolla, CA 94340 • 619/555-4975 • hansowan@xxx.com

CAREER OBJECTIVE

Commercial artist for an advertising agency.

SKILLS & ACCOMPLISHMENTS

- Produce line drawings for magazine advertisements, 35mm slides, and promotional materials.
- Experienced in watercolors, acrylics, airbrush techniques, and pastels.
- Handled all aspects of production, from concept to finished work.
- Experienced with 35mm color and black-and-white photography. Own Leica professional equipment and have extensive lighting facilities for studio shooting.
- Some experience with film stripping, taping, and masking.

EMPLOYMENT HISTORY

La Jolla Production Inc., La Jolla, CA
Commercial Artist, 1999 to Present

University of New Mexico, Albuquerque, NM
Staff Photographer, Department of Printing, 1997 to 1999

Coleman College, La Mesa, CA
Assistant, Design Department, Summers 1996 and 1997

EDUCATION

University of New Mexico, Albuquerque, NM
B.F.A. in Illustration and Painting; minor in Photography, 1997

REFERENCES

Available on Request

TANYA WELSH

2235 N. OAK STREET • IOWA CITY, IA 53340
(319) 555-5892 • CELL: (319) 555-6221 • TANYAWELSH@XXX.COM

CAREER OBJECTIVE

An entry-level position in the field of advertising,
preferably in the area of market research.

EDUCATION

University of Iowa, Iowa City, IA
B.S. degree in Advertising with minor in Marketing, expected December 2004
G.P.A.: 3.5 (overall) / 4.0 (major field)

PERTINENT COURSES

Advertising	Public Relations
Marketing Management	Industrial Marketing
Research Methods	Business Statistics
Marketing Research	Advertising Campaigns

EXPERIENCE

UNIVERSITY OF IOWA
College of Business
Research Analyst, 2002 to present

— Conduct surveys under divers conditions and among varied consumer
groups, including college students, retail store and motion picture patrons,
and heads of households.
— Compile data from various studies to form basis for national research
project on consumer spending potential for leisure products.
— Write summary reports on findings, including preliminary analysis.

THE DAILY IOWAN
University of Iowa Student Newspaper
Advertising Manager, 2001 to 2003

— Increased the number of regular advertisers from 12 to 22 over three
semesters.
— Eliminated paper's budget deficit through increased advertising revenue.
— Handled budgeting and payroll for staff of four commissioned sales
representatives.

ACTIVITIES

American Advertising Association, student chapter treasurer, Key Club, Service
Honorary Marching Band

References available on request

Dai Guillame

261 West First   daiguillame@xxx.com
Brooklyn, NY 11221   Telephone: (212) 555-2294

Objective

Seeking an entry-level position in advertising/marketing, with opportunity for advancement. Willing to relocate anywhere in the United States or overseas.

Academic Summary

Adelphi University, Garden City, New York
B.S. Advertising, Minor: Marketing and Public Relations
June 2002; GPA 3.2 (4.0)
Dean's List, five semesters

Relevant Experience

Brooklyn Borough Chamber of Commerce (Work Experience, Spring 2002)
- Worked with advertising agency to develop advertising campaign to promote corporate employment training opportunities.
- Designed two posters used for promoting industrial development opportunities.
- Wrote copy for public service announcements for radio and cable television.
- Recruited speakers for monthly Chamber meetings.
- Coordinated and distributed meeting agendas.
- Assisted Chamber Director in promoting organization's activities.

Small Business Administration (Internship, sponsored by Advertising Department, Adelphi University, Summer 2001), Garden City, New York
- Conducted demographics study of small businesses in Upstate New York.
- Presented study findings to Garden City Chamber of Commerce.
- Wrote summary report on study results, published in *New York Business* magazine.
- Wrote copy for, designed, and produced a pamphlet on services provided by the SBA for small business operators.

Public Relations and Development Office, Brooklyn General Hospital (Internship, Summer 2000)
- Prepared layout and edited text for three issues of *General News,* hospital newsletter for medical and support staff.
- Prepared community service advertisements for local newspapers to promote health care courses offered through the hospital.
- Attended seminar on hospital public relations.

Hope (Volunteer for nonprofit organization that helps handicapped individuals find employment, 1999 to present)
- Write press releases and public service announcements to seek employment opportunities and announce available services to qualified individuals.
- Work with management personnel to develop promotional strategies for reaching handicapped individuals.

References available upon request.

Angelique Brady

88 Park Lane
Baltimore, Maryland 21206
Telephone: (410) 555-2984
angeliquebrady@xxx.com

Job Objective:	To work in an advertising design position that will utilize my creativity, visual organization, and communication skills
Education:	University of Illinois, College of Fine and Applied Arts, Urbana-Champaign, IL Bachelor of Fine Arts in Industrial Design, May 2001
Relevant Courses:	Design Studio, Design Methodology, Materials Processing, Rendering, AutoCAD, Practical Physics, Advertising, and Photography
Activities:	Affiliate member, Industrial Designers Society of America
Employment Experience:	**2001 to present** **Brightwood Temporary Services, Baltimore, MD** • Accounts payable assistant • Chartered microfilming of invoices • Route sales auditor **Summer & Winter Breaks, 1997 to 2001** **Affiliated Bank of Baltimore, Baltimore, MD** • Bank teller • Managed currency, balanced figures • Data entry • Direct customer interaction
Honors:	Finalist, Baltimore Designers Guild Annual Competition Works exhibited at Krannert Art Museum, Urbana-Champaign, and Baltimore Designers Guild Gallery Dean's List, four semesters
References:	On request

Gillian K. Robinson
gillianrobinson@xxx.com

Current Address
1100 E. Grand, 1605B
Bloomington, Indiana 42167
(812) 555-6724

Permanent Address
55 W. Third Avenue
Houston, Texas 77054
(713) 555-5876

Objective *To obtain an advertising sales position with opportunities for advancement.*

Education REND LAKE COLLEGE, Ina, IL
Four semesters of core curriculum work
INDIANA UNIVERSITY, Bloomington, IN
Bachelor of Arts, Advertising with a minor in English
Anticipated December 2004. Current GPA 3.93/4.0

Honors INDIANA UNIVERSITY
• Selma Jane Rockfield Scholarship, IU College of Business
• Jefferson County Alumni Association Scholarship
• Admissions and Records Academic Scholarship
• Dean's List

REND LAKE COLLEGE, Ina, IL
• President's Scholarship
• Benton Business and Professional Women's Club Scholarship
• President's Honor List

Activities INDIANA UNIVERSITY
• Sigma Tau Delta, Advertising Honorary, Treasurer
• Member, Phi Kappa Phi, National Honorary
• Member, College of Business Honor Society
• Advertising Club, Membership Secretary

REND LAKE COLLEGE
• Member, Phi Theta Kappa
• Student Delegate, Rend Lake College Board of Trustees
• Student Representative, Campus and Facilities Committee
• Illinois Governmental Internship Program

Page 1 of 2

Work History   INDIANA UNIVERSITY
Tutor, Achievement Plus Program, 8/01 to present
• Tutor learning disabled college students in English.
• Assist in drafting, editing, and proofing essays.

Student Secretary, Chair, Department of Curriculum
and Instruction, 9/00 to present
• Type correspondence and other documents.
• Complete proofreading, editing, and revising of
  department documents.

REND LAKE COLLEGE
Student Assistant, Registrar/Admissions Office
9/98 to 6/00
• Performed computer data entry, student registration
  processing, and maintenance of student transcripts.
• Created and maintained correspondence and
  official documents.

Additional   Willing to travel and relocate. References on request.

Brian Bassist

1134 Valley Road • Flint, Michigan 62340

(606) 555-2849 • (606) 555-1003 • brianbassist@xxx.com

Objective	Partner in advertising agency specializing in corporate advertising
Education	Master's in Business Administration, Advertising Special Segment, UCLA, May 1995
	Postgraduate training through American Advertising Federation, 1999–2001
	Bachelor of Science, Advertising, with minor in Marketing, University of Michigan, Flint, June 1997
Consulting Experience	Consulted with Davis, Markham, and Howard on corporate advertising campaign strategy for six major national corporate accounts, 1997–2002.
	Independent consulting projects with three advertising agencies in the Detroit area in the fields of market research, identifying market niche, product positioning, and new product development, 1995–1997.
Advertising Expertise	Worked as Advertising Manager for Simmons Machinery, Detroit, MI, 1995–1997.
	Relevant course work in Advertising, Market Research, Consumer Behavior, Color Theory in Advertising, Business Statistics, Strategic Planning, Corporate Advertising, and Public Relations.
	Served as graduate instructor in Advertising at UCLA College of Business, 1992–1995.
Interpersonal Skills	Consistently received high performance appraisals from employees in anonymous evaluations at Simmons Machinery.
	Known for ability to interact with small and large groups as well as individuals.
	Elected student body president of University of Michigan for ability to represent a diversity of opinions and needs.

References on request

Yuri Uno

15 Front Avenue NW • Washington, D.C. 20120
201/555-2988 • yuriuno@xxx.com

OBJECTIVE

Seeking a position as Advertising Manager for a daily newspaper.

EXPERIENCE

Capitol Weekly
Washington, D.C.   **9/99 to present**
Advertising Sales Supervisor
Handle fifteen regular advertising accounts. Charged with developing client base. Developed sales strategies that posted net increases of 28% over the last two years. Increased regular advertiser inches by 18%. Work with design department to develop finished advertisements. Assist clients with concept development. Supervise staff of four sales representatives and support staff of two designers, two production artists, and three clerical workers.

The Tennessean
Nashville, TN   **9/97 to 8/99**
Advertising Sales Representative
Handled twelve major accounts for statewide daily newspaper. Maintained advertising sales records for entire sales group. Developed in-house advertisements to promote display ads to potential clients. Made sales presentations. Developed and implemented reader survey and prepared analysis for use in demographic fact sheet to send to current and potential advertisers. Received Top Salesperson of the Month award for three consecutive months.

Nashville School District
Nashville, TN   **2/89 to 8/97**
Director of Public Information
Responsible for the direction and management of the school district's public information and community relations program. Assigned and wrote articles on activities, events, and programs pertaining to education. Took and developed photographs for inclusion in newsletters and news releases. Submitted weekly news releases to local media. Prepared all district publication to camera-ready status for printing.

EDUCATION

University of Tennessee, Martin
Bachelor of Arts, Liberal Arts   1988

University of Maryland, Baltimore County   1997 to 1999
Continuing Education: Advertising, Business Management, Business Operations, Consumer Behavior, Applications in Business

References available on request.

JAMES ARTHUR KNOX

15829 Grant Avenue • Fargo, North Dakota 52289
(701) 555-9042 • jamesknox@xxx.com

OBJECTIVE

Seeking a position as assistant traffic manager for a major advertising firm. Able
to relocate anywhere in the United States.

EXPERIENCE

FARGO HERALD-TIMES   **9/00-present**
Fargo, North Dakota
Production Manager
Responsible for the design of advertising supplements, classified and display adver-
tisements using Macintosh computer. Set deadlines and timelines for completing
tasks associated with weekly newspaper.

SIR SPEEDY PRINT CENTER   **9/97-8/00**
Bismarck, North Dakota
Graphic Artist/Typesetter
Performed varied duties as they relate to the printing industry. Primary areas of
responsibility were typesetting on Macintosh with Linotronic 300 output, graphic
design on QuarkXPress and Adobe Illustrator, pasteup, stripping, and darkroom.
Also involved in customer service and some outside sales. Handled all equipment
maintenance and procurement.

INSTAGRAPHICS   **8/95-9/97**
Bismarck, North Dakota
Desktop Publishing Professional
Owned and operated small desktop publishing business. Made customer contact,
developed marketing plan and materials, made presentations, prepared original
designs based on client needs, and served as service bureau for other graphic
designers. Hired staff of designers, production assistants, typesetters, and darkroom
technicians. Coordinated with local print shop for quantity discounts.

EDUCATION

B.A. IN GRAPHIC DESIGN   **6/95**
Moore College of Art, Philadelphia, PA

A.A. IN PRINTING TECHNOLOGY   **6/92**
North Dakota State University, Fargo, ND

ADDITIONAL COURSE WORK IN ADVERTISING   **1997-1998**
North Dakota State University, Fargo, ND

References available on request

LAWRENCE P. DENNING

P.O. Box 2286
Iowa City, IA 52244
319/555-0029
lawrencedenning@xxx.com

OBJECTIVE

Classified advertising sales and data entry position, swing shift.

EDUCATION

Jefferson High School, Iowa City, IA
Expected graduation date, June 2003
Extensive course work in Journalism and Communications
Current G.P.A. 3.86

Planning to attend Iowa State University journalism program.

RELEVANT EXPERIENCE

- Worked on student newspaper advertising staff, calling on potential and current advertisers to sell advertising space.
- Performed data entry of classified advertisements.
- Computed word count and rates for classified ads.
- Performed word processing functions.
- Assisted with layout and pasteup of newspaper.
- Operated stat camera.

ACTIVITIES & ACHIEVEMENTS

- Awarded First Place in Editorial category in Iowa High School Journalism Competitions
- Placed Second in Photography category, IHSJ Competition
- Honor Roll
- National Honor Society
- Member, Student Chapter, Iowa Newspaper Publishers Association

REFERENCES

Available on request

JUDITH A. WASHINGTON   judithwashington@xxx.com

958 NW Sycamore • Amarillo, Texas 78077 • 806/555-0944

CAREER OBJECTIVES

To enhance advertising communication by utilizing computer graphics systems and/or traditional print media, and to work in a creative environment where my background in computers, graphics, and management will be used and further developed.

EXPERIENCE

Computer Graphics: Designed and produced drawings, charts, slides, video titles, large flip charts, newsletters, manuals, logos, ads, and brochures, using most major software programs on the Macintosh, IBM, and Amiga. Developed techniques and trained new employees in the use of computer graphics systems, evaluated and beta-tested hardware and software.

Production Management: Coordinated and supervised employees and freelancers in the creation of slides and manuals, and in newspaper production. Hired and trained employees, maintained budgets, planned for fluctuating workloads and deadlines. Developed more efficient production procedures. Interacted with suppliers and clients. Met deadlines. Maintained hard disk storage and tape backups, operated typesetting and stat camera equipment, ordered supplies. In traditional graphics, coordinated typesetting, photography, artwork, and printing on advertisements, brochures, newsletters, books, annual reports, catalogs, slides, and a newspaper.

Graphic Design: Translated concepts and information into appealing graphics, text, and images for advertisements, brochures, newsletters, charts, catalogs, packaging, newspaper ads, and video slides. Skilled in type specification, creative layout, technical drawing, and spot illustration.

Typography: Created computer typefaces for a computer typography program. Excellent knowledge of typography. Experienced with various typesetting programs and traditional typesetting machinery.

Darkroom: Produced high-quality stats, halftones, color keys, distortions, color separated negatives, and stripped film negatives.

JOB HISTORY

2001 - Present	Freelance: Presentation graphics, desktop publishing
1999 - 2001	Quality Printing Corporation, Palo Alto, CA
1997 - 1999	Prima Valley Publishing, Menlo Park, CA
1995 - 1997	Freelance: Graphic production and design
1992 - 1995	Graphic Productions, Menlo Park, CA
1989 - 1992	Flair Typographics, Itasca, IL
1987 - 1989	Art Packaging Corporation, Des Plaines, IL
1985 - 1987	Kingsbury Corporation, Des Plaines, IL

EDUCATION

1985, Bachelor of Arts Degree, Fine Art
Southern Illinois University, Carbondale, IL

References Available Upon Request

Ruth Solomon
330 Clarges Street, Apt. 24C
Salt Lake City, UT 84113
(801) 555-0938

Objective
To begin a career in advertising.

Education
Master of Arts in Journalism, The University of Iowa, Iowa City, May 2002
Area of Specialization: Advertising
GPA: 4.0

Courses

Advertising Copywriting	Advertising Planning
Media Relations	Public Relations Writing
Corporate Communications	Consumer Behavior
Advertising Design	Production Technology

Bachelor of Science in Fisheries, University of Idaho, Moscow, June 1989

Relevant Experience

August 1999 - 2002   Graduate Teaching Fellow, University of Iowa

July 1989 - August 1999   Fisheries Management/Information Research
(details available on request for curriculum vitae)

Activities
- Editor for International Association of Business Communicators, Utah Chapter.
- Master's project on developing advertising, public service announcements, and mail campaign for the Alliance for Environmental Education.
- Part-time proofreader of grant proposals and scientific reports, Iowa and Utah.
- Member, International Association of Business Communicators, Society for Technical Communicators, and Phi Eta Kappa Advertising Honorary.

References
Available at University of Iowa Career Placement Center and on request.

JEANETTE SCHUMACHER

89 W. Morgan Avenue • Milwaukee, Wisconsin 53100
(414) 555-0824 • jeanetteschumacher@xxx.com

JOB OBJECTIVE

Permanent part-time work in the graphic arts and production department of a large advertising agency. Long-term goals: complete a degree in advertising and design and obtain a full-time position in art direction.

EDUCATION

Associate in Science Degree in Visual Communications
Milwaukee Community College, 2002
Curriculum included design and character generation, process camera, presswork, typesetting, and black-and-white photography.

Currently enrolled in the undergraduate graphic design program with minor in advertising communications at the University of Wisconsin–Milwaukee.

EMPLOYMENT HISTORY

CAPITAL PRESS - Newspaper (1998 to Present)
Broad Street & First, Milwaukee, WI
Pasteup Artist/Typesetter
Responsible for pasteup of newspaper pages, including classified and special advertising sections. Typeset and pasteup display advertisements and news copy. Also work in Creative Department as typesetter, where I prepare forms, newsletters, brochures, and other outside jobs. Equipment: Macintosh, Adwriter, MycroComp Newstouch, LaserWriter II, Linotronic 300, Compugraphic Integrator/PowerPage, 8400 laser printer, film processor, page proofer. Also maintain equipment and chemicals.

ADVANCED TYPOGRAPHICS - Service Bureau (1996 to 1998)
335 Lake Blvd., Milwaukee, WI
Typesetter/Pasteup Artist
Typeset copy for magazine, newsletters, brochures, and advertisements. Pasteup of advertisements, newsletters, tabloid newspapers, and various other projects. Equipment: Compugraphic Integrator, 8400 laser printer, film processor.

MILWAUKEE GRAPHICS - Graphic Design/Service Bureau (1995 to 1996)
1156 Commercial St., Milwaukee, WI
Typesetter/Pasteup Artist/Process Camera Operator
Responsibilities included setting type, working with clients to select type fonts and styles appropriate to the job, preparing pasteup of publications and books, and camera work (PMTs, PMT halftones, line shots). Equipment: Compugraphic 7500, stat camera.

REFERENCES AVAILABLE ON REQUEST

Mary Elizabeth Bishop

462 Main Street, Apt. 1   303/555-4546
Durango, Colorado 81301   marybishop@xxx.com

Education   Fort Lewis College, Durango, CO
                       Advertising/Communications
                       Bachelor of Arts, 2001

Career Experience
9/99 - 1/01   *Rolling Stone* magazine, New York, NY
                       Research Intern
                       •Checked facts for publication
                       •Established positive rapport with professionals while preparing
                        and confirming copy
                       •Organized and maintained research library
                       •Edited and proofread copy

8/97 - present   *The Independent*, Fort Lewis College (FLC) Newspaper
                       Staff Member
                       •Awarded Writer of the Year 1999
                       •Writer of political, editorial, social, hard news, and features
                       •Production assistant duties include layout and pasteup
                       •Advertising sales
                       •Copyediting
                       •Typesetting

1/96 - 1/97   KRK Channel 4/FLC News
                       News Writer and Videographer
                       •Wrote, filmed, and edited weekly campus newscast

9/96 - 9/98   *Passages*, FLC Literary Arts Magazine
                       Assistant Editor (1996-1997)
                       Editor (1997-1998)
                       •Organized 12-member staff
                       •Obtained largest magazine budget in FLC history
                       •Established criteria and guidelines in selecting entries
                       •Maintained harmony with group decisions

Other Work
Experience   Admissions Assistant, Metropolitan Museum of Art, New York, NY
                       Library Aide, Fort Lewis College Library, Durango, CO

Skills   •Photography (black-and-white, color)
                       •Macintosh computer (graphics, page layout, word processing)
                       •NCR Computer (word processing, graphics)

Activities   •Scarlet Letters, FLC Communications Club
                       •Performed in FLC Theatre
                       •Volunteer at Burdett Center for the Aging

Carlos Diaz

836 Marshall Street
Trenton, New Jersey 08776
(609) 555-4310
carlosdiaz@xxx.com

Objective
Entry-level position as advertising copywriter with small to midsize agency.

Education
Newark College, Newark, NJ
B.A. in Communications with emphasis on Advertising, 2002

Accomplishments
- Worked as researcher in the advertising department of a major national magazine.
- Developed demographic profiles of magazine subscribers for advertiser information.
- Organized 12-member staff of advertising sales representatives for student newspaper.
- Oversaw all aspects of advertising department of student weekly newspaper.
- Determined and calculated ad space rates and frequency discounts.
- Wrote advertising copy for clients who lacked skilled staff writers.
- Worked with clients to develop advertising concepts.
- Produced a 10-ad series that won a regional advertising competition.
- Experienced in typesetting and copyediting for publication.
- Wrote news articles and feature stories for local media and student newspaper.
- Wrote, filmed, and edited weekly half-hour campus television news broadcast.
- Wrote, filmed, and edited television commercials for various student organizations.

Work History
- Advertising Manager, *The Newark News Week*, Newark College, Newark, NJ
- News Team, WNC-TV, Newark College, Newark, NJ
- Research Intern, Advertising Department, *Time* magazine, New York, NY

References
Available upon request.

SHARINA K. MYERS

5747 Pine Street SW • Shawnee, Oklahoma 74802
405/555-9371 • sharinamyers@xxx.com

OBJECTIVE

Seeking a position with the advertising department of a newspaper or magazine where my experience with writing, communications, and public relations may contribute to advertising sales as I gain new skills and reshape my abilities for a new career in advertising.

EDUCATION

University of Oklahoma, Norman, OK: Master of Arts, Journalism with emphasis in Advertising, 2001

University of Oklahoma, Norman, OK: Teacher Certification, English, 1994

Eastern New Mexico University, Portales, NM: Bachelor of Arts, English, 1992

Southwestern Oklahoma State University, Weatherford, OK: Bachelor of Arts, Journalism, 1990

PROFESSIONAL EXPERIENCE

The Quarter Horse Journal, **Amarillo, TX:**
Editorial Coordinator, January 1995 to August 2001
Coordinated staff and freelance reporters for semiannual journal. Oversaw copyediting, proofreading, and layout.

Maysville High School, Maysville, OK
Teacher, August 1990 to June 1995
Taught English, Journalism, Speech. Served as yearbook adviser and newspaper adviser. Graded essays for the state GED examinations.

The Southwester, **Southwestern Oklahoma State University, Weatherford, OK**
Reporter, January to June 1990/Advertising Salesperson, January to June 1989
Assigned articles to student reporters, wrote and edited articles for the paper, chose copy to include in each issue, assisted in layouts and headline writing. Took calls for advertising department to reserve ad space, developed advertising promotion ads and flyers to encourage sale of personal and business classified ads.

Public Relations Department, Southwestern Oklahoma State University
Reporter, September 1988 to May 1989
Conducted interviews and wrote press releases on various faculty members and students at the college to be published in local newspapers and distributed to hometown newspapers.

REFERENCES ARE AVAILABLE ON REQUEST

• Timothy Blaisdell

P.O. Box 216B3
Boise, Idaho 83702
208.555.8920
timothyblaisdell@xxx.com

• Education

University of Idaho, Boise, Master of Arts, 1999 Major: Advertising G.P.A. 4.0

Montana State University, Bozeman, Bachelor of Arts, 1993. Major: Journalism
G.P.A. 3.87

• Professional Experience

Advertising Director, *The Boise Sun*, Boise, ID   August 1998–present

Responsibilities: Develop advertisements and promotion materials for advertising clients. Conduct periodic reader surveys and analyze response with regard to demographics, marketing strategies, and subscription potential. Created ads that were directly responsible for producing $50,000 in additional advertising sales in a two-month period. Awarded two regional and one national American Newspaper Advertisers Association Honor Awards for in-house advertising design. Supervise staff of six advertising sales representatives and five graphic and production artists and typesetters.

**Marketing Coordinator, Continuing Education Department
University of Idaho   1995–1998**

Responsibilities: Planned and developed marketing strategy for attracting students to the university's summer term program. Wrote and designed promotional literature, including bulletins, brochures, advertisements, and public service announcements. Coordinated with designers, typesetters, photographers, service bureaus, media advertising sales representatives, and printers. Maintained advertising and promotion budget. Conducted surveys and evaluations.

Promotion Coordinator, *InterArts* Magazine, Boise, ID   1993–1995

Responsibilities: Coordinated all advertising sales for twelve-page display advertising section and two-page classified ad section. Made customer calls, developed ad rate cards and advertiser fact sheets, handled billing and collection. Scheduled self-promotion advertising and exchanged advertising with other publications. Maintained advertising budget.

• Honors

UI Graduate Teaching Fellowship, Journalism/Advertising, 1997–1998
UI Scholar's Award, 1998
MSU Scholarship and Leadership Award, 1992
MSU Dad's Club Scholarship, 1992

References available on request.

Edward G. McDonald

3 Battersea Street
Portland, Maine 04129
(207) 555-9365
edwardmcdonald@xxx.com

Objective

A position as an advertising account executive with a firm handling primary products and manufacturing accounts.

Experience

* Managed 34 national accounts for the timber, agriculture, and steel industries.
* Worked with advertising sales representatives from print and broadcast media to negotiate space rates for clients.
* Headed creative teams charged with developing corporate identity, advertising, campaign strategies, and sponsorship promotions.
* Designed and directed development of several advertising campaigns, two of which won national awards for both concept and net result.
* Experienced with analysis of demographic data and market survey reports.
* Created and implemented advertising, direct mail, and promotional campaigns.
* Initiated all advertising and sales promotional materials for U.S. Steel.
* Served as media buyer for a major New York advertising agency.

Work History

Haddon, Briden, and Walsh, Portland, ME
Associate Account Executive, 1999 – Present

Bacher Spielvogel Bates, Inc., New York
Advertising Account Assistant, 1995 – 1999

BBDO Worldwide Inc., New York
Media Buyer, 1994 – 1995

Roy Ross Group, Inc., Bloomfield Hills, MI
Advertising Assistant, 1991 – 1993

Education

Michigan State University, East Lansing, MI
B.A. in Business Administration, 1991
Emphasis: Advertising and Corporate Communications

References available on request.

Jerome Marcus

2235 E. 27th Street • Bronx, NY 10069 • 718/555-2875 • jeromemarcus@xxx.com

Objective

A position as an advertising assistant where I can use my planning, marketing, and design skills.

Skills & Experience

Handled four accounts for advertising agency.

Wrote copy, designed, and laid out advertisements.

Assisted with traffic control.

Served as liaison between clients and account executives.

Assisted in designing ads for magazine publication.

Computed ad sizes and rates.

Translated data from dummy production worksheets for distribution and review.

Assisted with market research survey development.

Implemented developments in advertising rate card and informational packet that directly contributed to increased advertising sales.

Work History

Advertising Intern, Bozell
New York, NY, Summer 2001

Advertising Assistant, part-time, *Manhattan Digest* magazine
New York, NY, 1998-2001

Classified Advertising Sales, *New York Daily News*
Long Island, NY, 1996-1998

Education

Bronx Community College, 2001 graduate
Major: Business and Advertising
GPA: 3.86 in major courses, 3.4 overall

Activities

President, Business Club
Vice President, Student Marketing Association
Treasurer, National Honor Society
Student Representative, Bronx District School Board
Volunteer, Central Bronx Hospice

TRENT GARRISON

335 La Paluma Blvd.
San Francisco, California 94136
415-555-3968
trentgarrison@xxx.com

OBJECTIVE

Video production specialist for large advertising production company.

SKILLS AND ACCOMPLISHMENTS

Won Golden Globe nomination for special effects production in documentary *L.A. Streets*.

Won Graphic Arts Best in Category Award for computer-generated animation series.

Won California Animation Society Award for computer-generated advertisement.

Produced more than 50 highly sophisticated animated advertisements for wide variety of corporate and industrial clients.

Designed and produced trademark and logo animation sequences for film corporations and television stations.

Assisted in creative design teams for special effects production in 17 major motion pictures.

Headed creative team for special effects production on two films.

EMPLOYMENT HISTORY

Industrial Light & Magic, San Jose, CA, 1996-2002
- Creative Team Leader, 1998-2002
- Design and Animation Production, 1997-1998
- Production Technician, 1996-1997

Videographics, San Francisco, CA, 1990-1996
- Production Department Manager, 1994-1996
- Animator, 1990-1994

EDUCATION

Pratt Institute, Brooklyn, NY
M.F.A., Video Arts and Computer Graphics, 1990

Marnie Valentine
427 Savanah Avenue
Savannah, Georgia 30292
(912) 555-9775
marnievalentine@xxx.com

Experience
- Assisted sales staff of advertising agency in areas of research and demographics.
- Prepared sales forecasts from available data.
- Identified potential target markets for new products.
- Worked with creative team to develop ad concepts and marketing strategies.
- Researched and compiled sales reports on consumer behavior patterns for a wide variety of products and services.
- Made professional presentation of advertising campaign proposals.
- Directed student advertising studio.
- Arranged filing and reporting systems on computer hardware.
- Organized department inventory.

Work History
Director, Advertising Studio, University of Georgia, Athens, GA, 1999-2002

Advertising Intern, Waite and Rand Associates, Savannah, GA, Summer 1999

Research Intern, Waite and Rand Associates, Savannah, GA, Summer 1998

Education
University of Georgia, Athens, GA
B.S. in Advertising, June 2002

Honors
Superior Service Award, Waite and Rand Associates, 1999
American Advertising Federation Merit Award,
Collegiate Regional Competition, 2000
Dean's List

References
On file with Career Center, University of Georgia, Athens, and on request.

Selina Morales

Present Address	**Permanent Address**
234 Lynn Rock Road	288 Monroe Drive
Kansas City, MO 64121	Winston, MO 64024
816/555-0567	selinamorales@xxx.com

Objective: Advertising copywriting

Education: University of Missouri, Kansas City, MO
Expected date of graduation, 12/03
Degree: B.A. in Advertising/Marketing minor

Work Experience: *Weekly Sentinel*, **Kansas City, MO**
(part-time, 9/01 to present)
Responsibilities include ad sales, ad copywriting, order handling, customer relations, data entry, and proofreading. Distribute checking copy to department heads.

The Kansas Advertiser, **Kansas City, MO**
(full-time, 6/99 to 9/01)
Special studies intern: responsibilities included design and layout of display advertisements, classified ad sales, and ad copywriting.

Related Course Work: Advertising Copywriting, Advertising Design, Advertising Campaigns, Public Relations Writing and Research, Electronic Design and Production, Business Communications, Newswriting

Activities: Sigma Delta Chi journalism honorary, Advertising Club, *Kansan* (university student yearbook) advertising sales and copyeditor, Pi Beta Phi national sorority

References and Portfolio are available on request.

QUENTIN SANTORINI

4325 Whitehall
Burlington, VT 05401
802-555-9876
quentinsantorini@xxx.com

JOB OBJECTIVE
A challenging entry-level position as a graphic artist in an advertising department or agency.

EXPERIENCE
▼ Produced drawings to illustrate magazine articles.
▼ Prepared computer graphic images for slide presentations.
▼ Developed promotional materials, including advertisements and brochures.
▼ Handled all aspects of production, from layout to finished product, for university publications office.
▼ Completed storyboards for television commercial series.
▼ Took photographs for publication in student newspaper.

EDUCATION
University of Vermont, Burlington, VT
B.A. in Illustration, May 2000

WORK HISTORY
Vermont Harvester Magazine, Burlington, VT
Commercial Artist, Summers 1998-2000 and full-time 2000-present

University of Vermont, Burlington, VT
Designer, University Publications Department, 1997-2000

Photographer/Production Assistant, Student Newspaper, 1996-1998

WORKSHOPS
Desktop Publishing with Microsoft Word, 2002
Graphic Arts on the Desktop, 2001
New England Design Seminar, 2001

Reference are available on request.

Juanita Rodriquez-Sutton

330 Hollywood Boulevard • Los Angeles, California 90063
(213) 555-2475 • (213) 555-0248 • juanitasutton@xxx.com

Career Objective

Seeking opportunity to put my marketing background and skills to work for a progressive advertising agency.

Experience

- Handled distribution, retail marketing, advertising, and mail-order marketing.
- Wrote advertising copy and distributed to clients and account executives.
- Obtained knowledge of domestic and overseas regulations for trademarks.
- Assisted marketing director with radio and television promotion and retail marketing.
- Coordinated radio and print interview opportunities for visiting artists and writers.
- Developed and implemented marketing plans for major retail chain.
- Directed research department for marketing data and sales reports.

Work History

LA Productions Weekly, **Los Angeles, CA**
- Marketing Director, 9/99 to Present
- Public Relations/Marketing Assistant, 6/98 to 8/99

KBOO Radio, Venice, CA
- Marketing and Promotions Director, 5/93 to 6/98
- Promotions Assistant, 3/92 to 5/93

Education

University of California, Los Angeles
- Postbaccalaureate study in Advertising and Marketing, 9/96 to 6/98
- Bachelor of Science in Journalism/Public Relations, 1/92

References are available upon request.

P. MARILYN PEDERSON

2274 Acorn Place
Santa Fe, NM 87538

marilynpederson@xxx.com
505.555.2176

CAREER OBJECTIVE
Seeking a challenging position as art director with a Santa Fe advertising agency.

EXPERIENCE
- Responsible for overseeing all projects in small advertising/typesetting studio.
- Handle all daily business.
- Supervise three typesetters and four artist/designers.
- Completed projects include: print media space advertisements, catalogs, P.O.P., direct mail, consumer, business to business, and recruitment advertising with a wide variety of accounts.
- Managed three-person art department.
- Supervised layout, design, illustration, storyboards, and production for corporate headquarters, financial, insurance, and travel sections.
- Handled overload from JC Penny store advertising department.
- As freelancer, provided designs to advertising department, automotive dealership, financial organizations, and advertising agencies.

WORK HISTORY
Creative Advertising Designs, Inc./Santa Fe   **1998-Present**
Senior Designer, Production Manager, Account Executive

Patterson & Associates, Marketing & Advertising Agency/Santa Fe   **1996-1998**
Designer, Production Manager

JC Penney Corporation, Corporate Advertising/New York   **1992-1996**
Senior Artist, Staff Artist, Production Assistant

Freelance Designer/New York   **1991-1992**

EDUCATION & SEMINARS
San Francisco Art Institute/California
Bachelor of Fine Arts Degree, Graphic Design & Illustration, 1991

How to Choose a Service Bureau/New York
Two-week seminar on printing specifications, purchasing, and related services, 1990

MEMBERSHIPS
Graphic Design Association/Santa Fe
American Association of Graphic Artists/National

REFERENCES are available upon request

SHAWN RIVER

2660 N. Grand • Billings, Montana 59105
406.555.5372 (days) • 406.555.3954 (cell)
shawnriver@xxx.com

CAREER OBJECTIVE

Seeking an assistant art director's position with an advertising agency that will utilize my skills in computer graphics and desktop publishing.

TECHNICAL SKILLS

design	layout	production art
illustration	copywriting	editing
typesetting	magazines	newsletters
display advertisements	flyers	posters
logos	letterheads	business cards
forms	reports	graphics

EQUIPMENT/SOFTWARE EXPERIENCE

Compugraphic EditWriter	AM Varityper equipment	IBM and Macintosh
Word	PageMaker	Microsoft Office
QuarkXPress	FreeHand	Adobe Illustrator
MacPaint	Adobe Photoshop	Harvard Graphics

EMPLOYMENT HISTORY

Graphic Plus, Billings, Montana. February 1995–present
Chief designer, editor, typesetter
- Prepare posters, design event-specific logos
- Produce brochures and other mailing pieces
- Handle all typesetting, design, and production functions for small design agency

A&S Typesetting, Billings, Montana. November 1989–January 1995
Production artist, typesetter
- Responsible for typesetting, layout, and pasteup
- Served as copywriter and ad artist for tabloid and magazine clients

Billings Printing Center, Billings, Montana. June 1983–November 1989
Production artist
- Provided clients with typesetting and clip art; produced advertising, newsletters, brochures, flyers, tabloids, and other products

EDUCATION

Montana Community College, Billings, Montana
Awarded two associate degrees in Printing Production (June 1983) and Graphic Design (January 1992)

Mariah Udey

11240 Paradise Way ■ Las Vegas, Nevada 89102 ■ (702) 555-2485
mariahudey@xxx.com

JOB OBJECTIVE

Obtain a position on a creative team with an advertising agency that will be challenging and use my background and skills in design, account representation, and strategic planning.

PROFESSIONAL EXPERIENCE

Swenson, Greves, and Huber Inc., Las Vegas   March 1999–Present
Senior Designer, Assistant Account Executive

■ Hold complete responsibility for four major accounts that I brought to the agency.
■ Participate on creative team for six major accounts.
■ Participate in corporate strategic planning.
■ Plan and balance client needs, goals, and budget considerations.
■ Direct staff and work with freelancers.
■ Provide press approvals and direct activity of graphics department.
■ Make recommendations to clients for long-term campaign strategies, concepts, and development.

Harrah's Club, Las Vegas   June 1992–February 1999
Advertising Department Manager

■ Planned and designed national advertising campaigns for major hotel and casino operation.
■ Worked extensively with television and radio production agency to develop broadcast ads.
■ Assisted with national advertising campaigns for major entertainment facility.
■ Designed and directed graphic artists in preparation of advertisements.

EDUCATION

University of Nevada, Las Vegas
Master's degree in Business Administration, 1992
Dual Bachelor's degrees in Graphic Design and Advertising, 1989

References available

PENNY MILLER HARRISON

1644 Craft Lane • Jersey City, New Jersey 07306
201/555-1197 • pennyharrison@xxx.com

OBJECTIVE

To join the advertising department of a large organization where my skills in marketing may be directed toward advertising.

EDUCATION

Master of Arts, Business Administration, June 2001
Stanford University, Stanford, California, G.P.A. 3.8

Relevant Courses

Business Administration	Organizational Dynamics
Marketing	Advertising Management
Advertising Copywriting	Financial Management
Policy and Procedures Planning	Legal Issues in Advertising
Research Methods	

Bachelor of Science, Design, May 1999
University of Pennsylvania, Philadelphia, G.P.A. 3.6

Relevant Courses

Graphic Design	Logo and Trademark Design
Advertising Design	Graphic Design Production
Typography	Packaging Design

EXPERIENCE

1997-present
New Jersey State Arts Foundation, Program Assistant
Designed flyers, posters, and advertisements announcing competitions. Served as administrative assistant to public art program coordinator. Researched other public art programs for policy development purposes. Prepared detailed reports on the program's operational effectiveness. Systematized slide registry and project files. Assisted in art and artist selection procedures. Coordinated selection committee meetings and slide presentations. Served as communication link between director, artists, and committees.

1995-1997
Composition Experts, Inc., Philadelphia, PA, Laser Printing Operator
Served as operator of computer source laser printers. Designed logos and forms using IBM/Xerox/Intran combination. Produced and distributed laser print and microfiche. Some programming and troubleshooting of laser printers.

HONORS

Summa cum laude, Stanford University
Phi Beta Kappa
Dean's Honors

References provided on request.

CAMERON D. FLYNN

2820 West Braddock Road
Alexandria, VA 22302
703.555.4761
cameronflynn@xxx.com

EMPLOYMENT OBJECTIVE

Advertising Account Executive with a growing, progressive advertising agency.

EMPLOYMENT EXPERIENCE

Virginia State Bank, Alexandria
Marketing/Advertising Director, 1999 - present

- Research target markets and competitive markets.
- Prepared complete marketing plans for introducing new line of bank services.
- Negotiate media space purchases in local news media.
- Coordinate production of television and radio commercials with contract production agency.
- Design artwork and coordinate production for posters, flyers, brochures, and advertisements.
- Design and prepare all in-house informational materials.

Alexandria Water and Electric Board
Advertising Coordinator, 1997 - 1999

- Prepared advertising plans for all changes in operations procedures or rates.
- Purchased advertising space in local print media.
- Designed and produced advertisements for publications.
- Coordinated production of quarterly 24-page newsletter to consumers.
- Sold advertising space in newsletter.

AccuPartners, Inc.
Computer Support Specialist, 1994 - 1997

- Provided instruction for clients in the use of accounting software.
- Provided basic accounting instruction and training in the preparation of income statements and balance sheets.
- Prepared reports with line specifications and custom features.
- Provided additional support for all software users.

Page 1 of 2

EMPLOYMENT EXPERIENCE (cont.)

Brentwood Stevens and Associates Inc.
Accountant, 1990 - 1994

• Collected data and prepared weekly, monthly, and yearly reports.
• Prepared cost and profit reports, generated revision reports.
• Communicated with banks and other financial institutions.

ACADEMIC BACKGROUND

Virginia Academy of Business
Associate Degree in Advertising, 1997

Alexandria Community College
Associate Degree in Accounting, 1990

REFERENCES AVAILABLE

Helena W. Greenlea

323 North Fountain Drive • Baltimore, MD 21225
301/555-8846 • helenagreenlea@xxx.com

Objective
Advertising Director for major publishing firm.

Recent Experience
Advertising Consultant, Berriman and Associates
Baltimore, MD. 1999 to present
Managing Director, advertising consulting firm for advertising departments of magazine and newspaper publishers, manufacturers, distributors, and entrepreneurs.

Management
Direct staff of creative advertising campaign managers, graphic artists, and advertising sales experts in providing consulting services to nationwide clients. Handle all budget, payroll, personnel, and management concerns.

Creative Solutions
Conceptualize management solutions for advertising departments of publishing firms, dealing with team strategy development, account management, and organization restructuring.

Marketing Strategies
Produce advertising campaign plans translating clients' information into concrete form and scheduling. Work closely with clients to help identify product markets, target advertising messages, and appropriate media delivery.

Art Direction
Direct creative work for print and film advertisements, brochure literature, books, publications, catalogs, posters, logos, trademarks, annual reports, labels and packages, slide programs, animated sequences, and games.

Advertising Manager, Holt, Rinehart & Winston
New York, NY. 1985 to 1999
Fifteen years of experience with all aspects of advertising for the nation's third largest book publisher. Also experienced with magazine division advertising programs, including advertising space sales.

Education
Bachelor of Science, Business Administration, 1984
Minor: Advertising and Marketing Promotions
Westminster College, New Wilmington, PA

References furnished on request.

Francine Masters

222 Market Street, NW
San Francisco, CA 94108
(415) 555-1232
francinemasters@xxx.com

Goal	To obtain a position as an assistant advertising account executive.

Work Experience

Advertising Coordinator, 1999-present
501 Union Center, San Francisco
- Coordinate media planning and buying for 20-store shopping center
- Research potential markets for ad campaigns
- Supervise artwork, layout, and production
- Handle sales promotions

Assistant Coordinator of Advertising, 1995-1999
Macy's, San Francisco, California
- Supervised trade shows and press shows
- Arranged and conducted sales meetings and presentations
- Designed and distributed press packets
- Developed marketing strategies
- Planned marketing and advertising campaigns
- Wrote and distributed press releases
- Served as liaison between clients and media representatives
- Acted as liaison to outside advertising agencies

Assistant Sales Manager, 1993-1995
Macy's, San Francisco

Education

Bachelor of Arts, Philosophy, 1993
Wesleyan University, Middletown, Connecticut

Honors

Junior Women's Scholarship
Dean's List
Senior Essay Award, Philosophy

References

Available on request.

STEWART SULLIVAN

OBJECTIVE

To secure a position on the production staff of an advertising agency where I may utilize my skills with graphic design, typesetting, and layout.

EXPERIENCE

Graphic Artist, Student Yearbook Staff, 1998-2002
- ▼ Assumed responsibility for overall design concepts in 212-page hardbound yearbook.
- ▼ Provided design assistance to editorial staff. Developed graphic elements for pages needing artwork.
- ▼ Designed page layouts and prepared camera-ready mechanicals for all advertising pages.
- ▼ Assisted in transfer from traditional layout and pasteup methods to computer page-layout technology with desktop publishing software.
- ▼ Prepared photographs for publication (cropped and sized).
- ▼ Supervised staff of production assistants.

Production Assistant, *Borah Gazette*, 1999-2002
- ▼ Prepared layouts for student newspaper.
- ▼ Cropped halftones.
- ▼ Designed graphics for accenting advertising section.

Typesetter, *Borah Gazette*, 1998-2000
- ▼ Input copy and headlines, choosing appropriate fonts, styles, and sizes.

EDUCATION

Borah Senior High School, Boise, Idaho
Class of 2002. Grade point average in art: 4.0

Areas of study: Journalism, Photojournalism, Graphic Design, Art (painting, drawing, watercolor, ceramics)

REFERENCES

Available on request.

1220 North Cole Road • Boise, Idaho 93709 • 208/555-2477 • stewartsullivan@xxx.com

WINSTON W. BRUSSARD, JR.

212 N. JEFFERSON STREET • ALBANY, GEORGIA 31701 • 706-555-4863
WINSTONBRUSSARD@XXX.COM

Objective

An ad sales position leading to a career in advertising management

Sales Experience

Served as salesperson in sporting goods store. Over six-month period, made consistent increases in sales, which led to my being selected as salesperson of the quarter, spring 2001.

Worked with advertising sales staff of student publications, both newspaper and yearbook. Made calls on local businesses, determined advertisement rates, and assisted with billing and bookkeeping.

Leadership

Elected Senior Class Vice President, 2001-2002. Responsible for overseeing committee; served as senior class representative to Student Senate. Assumed responsibilities of class President in her absence.

Revived Business Club; served as President, 1999-2002. Set meeting agendas, presided over meetings, instituted fund drive to sponsor professional visitations and field trips, organized trips to local business organizations.

Management

Managed Student Store, Monroe High School, 1999-2000. Supervised student clerks, scheduled work shifts, ordered supplies, received shipments and checked them against purchase orders, served customers.

Served as Weekend Night Manager at a 125-room motel. Greeted guests, managed registration desk, supervised night staff, and served as security representative on alternating weekends.

Work History

Weekend Night Manager, Motel Orleans, Albany, GA, July 2000-Present
Salesperson, Jefferson's Sporting Goods, Albany, GA, May 1999-June 2000
Advertising Sales, Monroe High School Student Publications, Albany, GA,
June 1998-May 1999

Education

Monroe High School, Albany, Georgia
Graduation class of 2002

Activities and Memberships: Business Club, Newspaper, Yearbook, Forensics Club, National Honor Society, Pep Club, Publicity Committee, Photography Club, JV and Varsity Wrestling

References

Available on request

VIRGINIA CONSTABLE

2248 WILLOW ROAD

LOUISVILLE, KY 40215-7682

502/555-8475

VIRGINIACONSTABLE@XXX.COM

JOB OBJECTIVE

To manage a creative advertising program for a small but growing computer technology firm.

EXPERIENCE

Self-Employed Creative Director, Louisville, KY
January 1999 to present
- Created an advertising and publications service company.
- Responsible for new business development.
- Managed seven statewide advertising accounts.
- Published a bimonthly, 28-page, full-color magazine for one client. Provided all copywriting, design, and production services as well as advertising sales and self-promotion ads.
- Assisted on production and advertising development for local business newspaper.
- Advertising development, sales, and production account for approximately 40% of activity.

Director of Advertising, Westport International, Louisville, KY
November 1997 to March 1999
- Coordinated all national and regional advertising efforts for this international clothing retailer.
- Supervised all creative development and broadcast production through a contract agency.
- Developed all collateral print production.
- Supervised regional media buying for 58-store cooperative.
- Responsible for local store marketing efforts for 36 Midwest franchise-operated stores.
- Created all corporate self-promotion materials.
- Developed community ties through sponsorships of local organizations.
- Trained all new franchise owners and store manager on in-store marketing and advertising.

Page 1 of 2

Media Buyer, Westport International, Louisville, KY
September 1995 to November 1997

- Served as media buyer for company-owned outlets in Kentucky.
- Television and radio buyer for the Midwest Regional Marketing Association Co-op.
- Conducted regional and national image and awareness survey.
- Developed, produced, and implemented an in-store customer response survey.
- Evaluated all company store sales results from target advertising campaigns.

EDUCATION

University of Kentucky
Bachelor of Arts, Business and Management, 1995
Minor: Communications/Advertising

ACTIVITIES

- Board of Directors, Mid-Kentucky Advertising Association
- Speaker, University of Kentucky Career Fair
- Woodie Award Recipient, Excellence and Achievement Award, seven awards from 1995 to 2001
- American Advertising Federation member since 1994

References are furnished on request

Jasmine Kiloiku

4423 Kilauea Avenue   **Honolulu, HI 96819**   **808-555-4378**
jasminekiloiku@xxx.com   **Cell: 808-555-7722**

Objective   Account Assistant with a midsize advertising agency

Experience   **Benton Simmons Matea & Foley, Inc., Honolulu, HI**
                        1999 to present
                        Display Advertising Media Buyer

                        Technical knowledge of advertising, design, pre-press, and printing functions. Experienced in budgeting, pricing strategies, and proposal writing. Coordinate all local advertising for seven major corporate clients. Through market analysis, identified prime media outlets and pursued advantageous advertising contracts for several clients.

                        Kaui Container Corporation, Honolulu, HI
                        1997 to 1999
                        Marketing and Promotion Coordinator

                        Organized and produced special events. Prepared all advertising and promotion materials. Produced quarterly design awards program. Participated in development of Kaui sales literature. Designed sales presentations using computer graphic presentation software on Macintosh. Planned and implemented effective advertising, public relations, and dealer incentive programs.

Education   Bachelor of Arts, Liberal Studies, 1997
                        Hawaii Pacific College, Honolulu, HI

References   Furnished on request

JAMES MARCHINGTON

15829 First Avenue
Battle Creek, MI 49017
(616) 555-9042
jamesmarchington@xxx.com

OBJECTIVE

Seeking a position as assistant production manager for a Chicago-area advertising firm.

EXPERIENCE

BATTLE CREEK REPORTER   Battle Creek, MI   9/99 to present
Production Manager

- Responsible for the design of advertising supplements, classified and display advertisements.
- Experienced with page layout on the Macintosh computer.
- Set deadlines and timelines for completing tasks associated with weekly newspaper.
- Supervised crew of production artists, photographers, and designers to ensure timely, quality production.

MICHIGAN PRINT CENTER   Battle Creek, MI   9/98 to 8/99
Graphic Artist/Typesetter

- Performed varied tasks related to the printing industry.
- Primary areas of responsibility are typesetting on Macintosh with Linotronic 300 output.
- Produced page layout and graphic design on QuarkXPress and Adobe Illustrator.
- Assisted with pasteup, stripping, and darkroom preparation.
- Involved in customer service and some outside sales.
- Handled all equipment maintenance and procurement.

GRAPHICS PLUS   Detroit, MI   8/94 to 9/98
Desktop Publishing Assistant

- Worked for small desktop publishing business.
- Made customer contact, developed marketing plan and materials.
- Made presentations and prepared original designs based on client needs.
- Output products prepared by other graphic designers.

EDUCATION

A.A. IN GRAPHIC PRODUCTION TECHNIQUES   June 1994
Sanders College of Art, Detroit, MI

A.A. IN PRINTING TECHNOLOGY   June 1992
Michigan State University, East Lansing, MI

ADDITIONAL COURSE WORK IN ADVERTISING   1997 & 1998
Michigan State University, East Lansing, MI

MICHELLE A. SUTTER
P.O. Box 18
ANN ARBOR, MI 48106
(313) 555-3758
michellesutter@xxx.com

OBJECTIVE
Seeking a position as an advertising market analyst.

EXPERIENCE
Hutchinson Computer Corporation, Ann Arbor, MI, 1996-Present
- Senior Sales Support Analyst, 2000-Present
- Field Marketing Specialist, 1999-2000
- System Analyst, 1996-1999

Directed development of marketing strategies, new product development, and advertising and promotion planning. Coordinated all aspects of high-level corporate visits for prospective customers requiring site participation by management and marketing division directors. Supervised corporate sales force of 128 sales representatives nationwide.

Intel Systems Corporation, Rapid City, SD, 1992-1996
- Customer Support Manager
- Support Analyst

Delivered product presentations and demonstrations. Designed and wrote product marketing guides, competitive reports, and training manuals for field sales and service representatives. Responsible for software installation, applications support, troubleshooting, and maintenance for 25 accounts.

Computer Technology Associates, Madison, WI, 1988-1992
- Educational Service Representative
- Sales and Marketing Representative

Presented sales demonstrations and negotiated equipment sales. Assisted with sales office activities.

EDUCATION
University of Wisconsin, Madison
- B.S. in Business Administration, 1988
- Minor: Advertising and Marketing

REFERENCES AVAILABLE

Tawana Mitchell

427 Portland Avenue, No. 22
Bridgewater, MA 02324
(508) 555-9775
tawanamitchell@xxx.com

Job Sought
Entry-level position in the field of advertising account management.

Experience
Director, Advertising Studio, University of Chicago, Chicago, IL, 2000-present
Direct student advertising studio. Work with creative team to develop ad concepts and marketing strategies. Create professional presentation of advertising campaign proposals. Organize department inventory.

Advertising Intern, Faulk & Strand Associates, Chicago, IL, Summer 2000
Assisted sales staff of advertising agency in areas of research and demographics. Prepared sales forecasts from available data. Identified and researched potential target markets for new products.

Research Intern, Faulk & Strand Associates, Chicago, IL, Summer 1999
Researched and compiled sales reports on consumer behavior patterns for a wide variety of products and services. Developed computer-based filing and reporting systems.

Education
University of Chicago, Chicago, IL
Bachelor of Science degree in Advertising

Honors & Activities
Superior Service Award, Faulk & Strand Associates, 1999
American Advertising College Honor Award,
   Collegiate National Competition, 1998
Dean's List
President, Student Council on Equality
Appointed to the Chancellor's Committee for the Status of Women
Served on University of Chicago Advertising Department Faculty Search Committee

References
On file with Placement Board Office, University of Chicago, and on request.

SANDER FELDSTEIN

Objective
A position as advertising account executive in Raleigh, North Carolina, area.

Experience
Haddon, Briden, and Walsh, Portland, Michigan
Associate Account Executive, 1999-present
- Manage 34 national accounts for the agriculture, packaging, and garment industries.
- Work with advertising sales representatives from print and broadcast media to negotiate space rates for clients.
- Head creative teams charged with developing corporate identity, advertising campaign strategies, and sponsorship promotion.

Bacher Spielvogel Bates, Inc., New York
Advertising Account Assistant, 1994-1999
- Designed and directed development of several advertising campaigns, two of which won national awards for both concept and net result.
- Experienced with analysis of demographic data and market survey reports.
- Created and implemented cooperative advertising, direct mail, and promotional campaigns.

BBDO Worldwide Inc., New York
Media Buyer, 1988-1994
- Initiated all advertising and sales promotional materials for U.S. Steel.
- Served as media buyer for major New York advertising agency.

Roy Ross Group, Inc., Bloomfield Hills, Michigan
Advertising Assistant, 1985-1988
- Provided analysis of demographic data and developed market survey reports.
- Assisted with advertising, direct mail, and promotional campaigns for wide range of clients.

Education
Michigan State University, East Lansing, Michigan.
B.A. in Business Administration, 1985
Emphasis: Advertising and Corporate Communications

References available on request

283 Durham Street • Durham, North Carolina
(919) 555-9365 • sanderfeldstein@xxx.com

Stephen Tyrol

330 Copley Road   Akron, OH 44308   (206) 555-2475
stephentyrol@xxx.com

Objective

A career in advertising account management

Related Career Experience

MidWest Clothiers, Akron, OH
Marketing Assistant Director, 9/98 to present
Public Relations/Marketing Assistant, 6/96 to 9/98

- Handle distribution, retail marketing, advertising, and mail-order marketing.
- Write advertising copy and distribute to advertising executives.
- Obtain knowledge of domestic overseas regulations on trademarks.
- Developed and implemented marketing plans for major retail chain.

WIJO TV/WGMA FM Radio, Boston, MA
Marketing and Promotions Assistant, 5/92 to 6/96
Research Assistant, 3/89 to 5/92

- Assisted marketing director with radio and television promotion and retail marketing.
- Coordinated radio and print interview opportunities for visiting artists and writers.
- Directed research department for market data and sales reports.

Education

University of Ohio, Akron
Advanced course work in Advertising and Marketing,
    9/88 to 6/90
Bachelor of Science degree in Marketing, 1/89

References are available upon request.

Sample Cover Letters

This chapter contains many sample cover letters for people pursuing a wide variety of jobs and careers in advertising.

There are many different styles of cover letters in terms of layout, level of formality, and presentation of information. These samples also represent people with varying amounts of education and work experience. Choose one cover letter or borrow elements from several different cover letters to help you construct your own.

FREIDA M. CARTER

335 W. Fifth Street
Brooklyn, NY 12009
718/555-5375
freidacarter@xxx.com

June 30, 20—

Ms. Linda Donaldson
Personnel Director
Brooklyn Savings Bank
12 South Main Street
Brooklyn, NY 12008

Dear Ms. Donaldson:

I am a recent graduate of Brigham Young University and am interested in working for the advertising department at Brooklyn Savings Bank. Ms. Abrams, the advertising director, told me to submit my resume to you for formal application.

As Ms. Abrams will tell you, I spent one summer working in the bank's advertising department as a student intern. I found the work challenging, exciting, and an ideal match for both my academic background and professional interests.

I would like to speak with you at your convenience to discuss employment opportunities and my qualifications. I am available at the number above most mornings before 11:00. Thank you very much for your time.

Sincerely,

Freida M. Carter

JAMILLA STEWART-LAWRENCE

125 W. Hollis Ave., No. 6
Charlotte, NC 28230
(704) 555-2789
jamillastewart@xxx.com

April 2, 20—

Susan St. James
Personnel Manager
IBM Corporation
22 West Corporate Parkway
Charlotte, NC 28238

Dear Ms. St. James:

In response to the notice posted at the University of North Carolina Career Center, I am writing to apply for the promotion/advertising position in your marketing department. After two years of experience in advertising and public relations, I know I can make a significant contribution to your company.

Most recently, I worked as advertising coordinator for University Savings Bank. I'm skilled in copywriting, ad design, and layout. One of my current responsibilities is publishing the company newsletter; consequently, I have become extremely familiar with WordPerfect word processing and both PageMaker and Ready, Set, Go desktop publishing applications. Additionally, I was responsible for developing advertising and promotional ideas for new products and grand openings.

As you'll notice from my resume, I also have experience writing for both television and radio. I would like you to put my varied background and skills to use in your company, and I look forward to your campus visit next month, when I would welcome the opportunity to show you my portfolio. I hope to talk with you soon.

Sincerely,

Jamilla Stewart-Lawrence

Richard Chin
4365 Woodruff Ave #45
Lakewood, CA 90713
richardchin@xxx.com

February 25, 20—

Mr. Paul Gill
ARL Publishing Group
Los Angeles, CA 90713

Dear Mr. Gill:

I am responding to your ad in Sunday's paper regarding the Advertising Production Coordinator position. I have been working in the graphic design field for the past three years and have completed a wide range of projects involving ad creation, development, and design.

I feel my creative style, my computer expertise, and my dedication to being the best that I can be make me a viable candidate for your position. My specific experience as the production coordinator for a printing firm gives me far more than the basic requirements.

My resume is enclosed. I hope we can arrange a time for an interview to explore potential opportunities. Thank you for your consideration.

Sincerely,

Richard Chin

554 20th Street, Apt. 22
Philadelphia, PA 19104
March 30, 20—

Ms. Maryann Fuller
Ketchum Communications
Six PPG Plaza
Pittsburgh, PA 15222

Dear Ms. Fuller:

I am writing to inquire about the advertising sales opening at Ketchum Communications. I spoke with your advertising manager, Mr. Fred Hughes, who suggested I send my resume to you in application for the position.

I will graduate from the University of Pennsylvania in June with a Bachelor of Arts in Communication, and I am eager to begin my career in the advertising field.

I completed an internship last year in the public relations department of A. Martin, Inc. My responsibilities there included assisting the staff in market and product research, demographics, and psychographics, and advertising concept and strategy planning. This practical experience, combined with an education that honed my copywriting and communications skills, provides qualifications that will be a plus for your organization.

Thank you for reviewing the enclosed resume. I will contact you next week in order to arrange a future meeting at your convenience.

Sincerely,

Karl P. Welch

879 Hawthorne Street
Melrose Park, IL 60164

April 13, 20—

Larsen Communications
2315 North Valley
Chester, IL 60646

Subject: Advertising design position

I am writing in response to your ad in the Sunday *Tribune*, and am enclosing a resume, which outlines my previous employment and education relevant to the advertising design position with Larsen Communications.

I have acquired many valuable skills from my work experience and education in the communications and design fields. I have used PageMaker and QuarkXPress, paired with design logic and sketching skills, to develop designs for products. As PR Manager at Talbott, Inc., I was responsible for all public relations and promotion, which included supervising all advertising accounts.

I would like an opportunity to discuss my qualifications and interest in your organization, and I can be reached at 847.555.1222 or via e-mail at kristinerabinski@xxx.com. I appreciate your time and consideration, and look forward to hearing from you.

Sincerely,

Kristine Rabinski

Gloria Santos

225 Delgado Street
Santa Fe, NM 87501

25 April, 20—

Ms. Barbara Savoy
Allegre Advertising Agency
3990 Paseo del Sol
Santa Fe, NM 87501

Dear Ms. Savoy:

I am writing at the suggestion of Marilyn Sander, the head of graphic design in your agency. She mentioned the possibility of current openings in account management.

I have recently relocated to Santa Fe and am looking for work in the advertising and promotion field. My skills and interest lie in the development and coordination of advertising campaigns. While managing the advertising department of New England Alliance, I developed concepts, designed ads, supervised layout and typesetting, and coordinated all media placement.

My training in communication and design is extensive, and my experience has prepared me for successful interactions with clients, coworkers, design staff, and production managers, all the people who must work together to make a campaign happen.

Please review the enclosed resume. I would like to meet with you at your convenience. Thank you for your time and consideration.

Yours truly,

Gloria Santos

Marcus J. Reed

259 W. North Avenue
Baltimore, MD 21202

---

18 April 20—

Vera Hampton
Advertising Director
Publicity Specialists, Inc.
7432 Orleans Street
Baltimore, MD 21231

Dear Ms. Hampton:

I am writing to inquire about current position openings involving graphics and advertising with your firm. I noticed your general employment announcement in the Career Center at Maryland University, where I am currently a graduating senior.

The enclosed resume outlines my managerial experience, as well as my strong background in product advertising, both in developing advertising campaigns and in design. Prior to returning to Maryland University, I worked for twelve years as a designer and account manager for a small design firm that specialized in advertising.

I am interested in a meeting to discuss my capabilities, and will call you next week to inquire about setting up an interview. Thank you for your consideration.

Sincerely,

Marcus J. Reed

Janis L. Gould
593 Rampart Ave.
Akron, OH 44313

30 March 20—

L. Conner
Capitol Communications
359 Main Street
Akron, OH 44308

Dear L. Conner:

I write in reference to your advertisement for an Advertising Director, which appeared in the March 28th edition of *NewsTime*. I believe my background and experience are well-matched to your needs.

My broad education and work record evolved from employment with ad agencies, design studios, publishing companies, newspapers, corporate art departments, and a TV station. As a freelance graphic artist/desktop publisher, I have acquired experience with a wide variety of organizations. I have created and produced advertisements and have also developed and implemented national advertising and publicity campaigns.

I would like to discuss the position further, and I will telephone you early next week to set up a possible meeting at your convenience. Thank you for your consideration.

Sincerely,

Janis L. Gould

JUDITH A. WASHINGTON   judithwashington@xxx.com

958 NW Sycamore • Amarillo, Texas 78077 • 806/555-0944

28 November 20—

Thomas V. Walker
President
Dallas Dimensions, Inc.
14 East Patterson
Dallas, Texas 75221

Dear Mr. Walker:

I was delighted to receive notification of the availability of the Production
Manager's position at Dallas Dimensions. Having visited your offices on
several occasions, I have been tremendously impressed with your facilities
and the organization's professionalism.

In reply to your kind note, I would like to submit the enclosed resume and
letters of recommendation for your consideration. The variety of projects I've
handled and the range of clients I've served during my years as a freelancer
will, I believe, place me in an advantageous position to contribute significantly
to your company's future growth.

I look forward to having an opportunity to talk with you further about the
position, the challenges it will provide, and the expertise with which I am
prepared to meet those challenges. I will telephone you early next week to
set up a time at your convenience. Thank you again for letting me know about
the opening.

Best regards,

Judith A. Washington

• Timothy Blaisdell

P.O. Box 216B3
Boise, Idaho 83702
208.555.8920
timothyblaisdell@xxx.com

12 October 20—

Director
Rocky Mountain Magazine
P.O. Box RM
Denver, Colorado 80201

Dear Sir/Madam:

In response to your recent advertisement in *AdWeek*, I would like to submit my professional resume for the position of Advertising Director.

My current role as Advertising Director of the daily newspaper *The Boise Sun* has provided tremendous challenges over the past seven years, but I am interested in exploring new growth opportunities, and magazine advertising is the natural next step. I have also held positions in marketing and promotion, and those skills appear to be high on your list of qualifications for the position.

Although currently living in Boise, I am quite happy to travel to Denver to talk with you at your convenience. I will call you early next week to inquire about your schedule. Thank you for considering the enclosed resume.

Yours sincerely,

Timothy Blaisdell

■ RICHARD WALKER

2774 Tower Drive, Chicago, IL 60647   **(312) 555-8831**
richardwalker@xxx.com   **(312) 555-6655**

September 24, 20—

T. Barker
Jameson Publishing Group
2261 S. Queen Street
Chicago, IL 60635

Dear T. Barker:

I am writing in response to your recent advertisement in the *Chicago Tribune* for an advertising production/promotion coordinator. I am very interested in the position, for this appears to be the challenge and opportunity I seek in the field of production and design.

In addition, I believe I'm right for the job. The enclosed resume provides the details, but the following professional highlights from my record are in keeping with your position requirements:

• Six years as a graphic artist and designer
• Three years experience in advertising design and production
• Expert with desktop publishing software and hardware
• Eight years management and supervisory experience

Along with my extensive professional background, I have kept current with the vast changes occurring throughout the electronic design, publishing, and pre-press industries, and can confidently say that I am at the high end of the learning curve.

Thank you for your consideration, and I look forward to having an opportunity to share with you a portfolio of my work.

Sincerely yours,

Richard Walker

Cheryl Scott

1590 Junction Boulevard • Lexington, KY 40506

May 15, 20—

Advertising Manager
Dodd Brothers Advertising
44 West Benchley
Lexington, KY 40509

Dear Sir or Madam:

I recently received notification through the University of Kentucky School of Journalism that you are looking for qualified advertising copywriters. Please accept the enclosed resume in application for one of these positions.

As a graduate of the graduate journalism program at the University of Kentucky, I have received extensive training in the field of advertising, including the opportunity to serve as the Advertising Coordinator for the university's public relations office. In this capacity, I have been responsible for directing and developing all advertisements and promotional materials, including radio and television commercials, newspaper and magazine display ads, brochures, posters, and flyers. I have written the copy for everything that has come out of the office since January of 1996.

I would appreciate an opportunity to share some examples of the past two years' productivity. I believe you will find my background and experience fully qualify me for the position of advertising copywriter. I look forward to talking with you.

Sincerely,

Cheryl Scott

Gary A. Azukas

2245 Haven Street   (207) 555-9197 (days)
Rumford, Maine 04276   (207) 555-2983 (evenings)
                              garyazukas@xxx.com

March 5, 20—

John Garcia
Advertising Director
WMTV
5 Broadcast Lane
Portland, ME 04277

Dear Mr. Garcia:

I am writing to inquire about the position of assistant advertising director listed in the March edition of *Broadcast News*. If the position is still vacant, I would very much like to apply. My professional resume is enclosed.

As my resume indicates, I have five years of experience with video production and editing for an organization that develops television commercials and documentaries for a wide range of clients. I have also been on the buying end of television advertising, as well as involved with developing market information with which to make strategic plans for television advertising campaigns.

After giving you an opportunity to review the enclosed resume, I will give you a call late next week to see about setting up a time when we can talk further about both the position and my qualifications. Thank you very much for your consideration.

Sincerely,

Gary A. Azukas

Morgan S. Thompson-West

October 14, 20—

Ruth McLennan
United Airlines
Corporate Advertising Division
1100 Madison Avenue, 20th Floor
New York, NY 10028

Dear Ms. McLennan:

In response to your recent advertisement in the *New York Times* for a print advertising art director, I am enclosing a brief resume and some samples of the well-known trademarks that I have been responsible for in previous employment.

During the past four years I have handled corporate identity, product development, advertising, and collateral for such clients as JFK International Airport, WBTM-TV, Brooklyn Medical Association, and Eastside Event Center. I have also provided creative services to New York National Savings Bank, Raymond Insurance Agents, and agencies such as Lyle Branett, P. Richard Thompson, and Tracy & Associates.

My strengths lie in creativity, print production, and management—essential skills for the advertising art director for a major corporation. I hope we can arrange an interview at your convenience to discuss what challenges the position offers and the skills and experience I can bring to your organization.

With best regards,

Morgan S. Thompson-West
2820 W. 57th Street
New York, NY 10019
212-555-6685
morganthompson-west@xxx.com

Mary E. Glancey

72 College Street • Beloit, Wisconsin 53511
(606) 555-4267 • maryglancey@xxx.com

March 17, 20—

Mr. Albert Quentin, Manager
Advertising Department
The Beloit Weekly
Second Avenue & Market Street
Beloit, WI 53511

Dear Mr. Quentin:

As a recent graduate of Beloit College, I am preparing to pursue a career in advertising and publishing. I would like to apply for the advertising copy-writer's position announced in the *Sunday Times*.

At Beloit, I served as Advertising Coordinator for the college newspaper, which had a readership of approximately 4,000. I was responsible for ad sales and ad production. Because it was such a small paper, I was often involved in many aspects of publishing, including newswriting, layout, advertising design, and production. This experience, along with my strong eye for detail, an ability to read quickly and efficiently, and my computer proficiency, would prove valuable to your organization.

I am enclosing a resume with more specific descriptions of my qualifications. I will furnish references on request. Thank you for your time.

Sincerely,

Mary E. Glancey

JAMES MARCHINGTON

15829 First Avenue
Battle Creek, MI 49017
(616) 555-9042
jamesmarchington@xxx.com

February 12, 20—

Carolyn Wheatley
Personnel Director
Denby & Associates
4317 Market Street, Suite 117
Chicago, IL 60619

Dear Ms. Wheatley:

I am responding to your recent advertisement for an assistant traffic manager. Enclosed with this letter of introduction is my resume, which will give you an overview of my education and experiences. I am sure you will find my background suited to your needs.

I hold two associate degrees in graphic design and printing. This diversified education prepared me for employment with several printing organizations, leading to my current role as Production Manager of the *Battle Creek Reporter*, Michigan's second-largest newspaper. As production manager, I am involved in many facets of the publishing process and have gained extensive experience in employee supervision and public relations.

I look forward to the opportunity to meet with you to discuss my qualifications further. I will call your office next week to arrange a possible meeting. Thank you for your time and consideration.

Sincerely,

James Marchington

Edward G. McDonald

3 Battersea Street
Portland, Maine 04129
(207) 555-9365
edwardmcdonald@xxx.com

26 July 20—

Corporate Director
Box 246C
c/o *Maine Herald*
845 Jefferson Avenue
Portland, ME 04129

To the Agency Director:

In reply to the advertisement posted in the July 18 edition of the *Maine Herald*, I would like to apply for the position of advertising director.

My interest in your advertisement was piqued by the description of your company as involved with primary products manufacturing. I have 13 years' experience as an advertising specialist, working primarily with timber, agriculture, and steel producers. My background includes work with print media, and I have won national awards for both advertising concepts and the results achieved by two different advertising campaigns.

I would like to have an opportunity to learn more about your organization and how my expertise can make a positive contribution to your advertising efforts. Please telephone me at your convenience. I am available at (207) 555-9365 most mornings or any time via e-mail at edwardmcdonald@xxx.com. Thank you for your time and attention.

Sincerely,

Edward G. McDonald

jolene e. marks

3335 North Road • Bellevue, Colorado 80512 • 303-555-4886
jolenemarks@xxx.com

June 15, 20—

Director of Advertising Sales
Finley Stern, Inc.
32 Boulder Avenue
Denver, Colorado 80236

Dear Director:

I am writing to you because I believe my education, work experience, and interests would make me an asset to your advertising sales department. If you anticipate any job openings in the near future, please consider my resume in application for a position in advertising sales.

I recently graduated from Colorado State University with a bachelor's degree in Journalism. My major course work in advertising and design, advertising copywriting, and publication management was supplemented with business courses in marketing, sales, and planning.

Beyond my education, I have practical experience. To put myself through college I took a clerical job at a local magazine. Seven months later I became the magazine's advertising sales representative and held that position for another two years. Because the magazine was a small one, I also worked on all aspects of the publication, from writing and editing to design, production, and circulation. It was there that I first began to test the skills I was learning in college.

This experience helped me to win an internship last summer, during which I worked as an advertising account assistant for a company that represents over 25 national corporations. I assumed immediate responsibility for two regional corporate accounts.

If you feel there may be a place for me at Finley Stern, I would be delighted to further discuss how my qualifications might be of value to you. I look forward to hearing from you.

Yours truly,

Jolene E. Marks

Christina Benson
33 West Arthur Place
Boca Raton, Florida 33486

November 18, 20—

Advertising Sales Manager
Boca Raton News
P.O. Box 1219
Boca Raton, FL 33481

Dear Sir or Madam:

I will graduate from Florida Atlantic College School of Journalism next month, and I would like to apply for a position in advertising sales with the *Boca Raton News*.

I am currently working part-time at the *Advertiser*, but would very much like to seek full-time work with an opportunity to expand my sphere of activity to include display advertising as well as classifieds. My experience as the advertising manager of the student newspaper at Florida Atlantic College has given me the skills and salesmanship I believe you are looking for.

My term will end November 29, and I will call you early in the following week to see if there might be a convenient time for us to meet and discuss the position further. If you would like to reach me in the meantime, I am available most afternoons at 555-2756 or by e-mail at christina benson@xxx.com. Thank you for your consideration in reviewing the enclosed resume.

Sincerely,

Christina Benson

Ian P. Robinson

1009 Selby Drive, Geneva, Illinois 60134
Home (630) 555-9984 • Work (630) 555-0228
ianrobinson@xxx.com

August 26, 20—

Director
Benchley, Faber & Associates, Inc.
P.O. Box 2568-D
Chicago, IL 60629

To the Director:

Please accept the enclosed resume in application for the Advertising Account Manager position announced in the August 20 issue of the *Chicago Sun-Times*.

Perhaps the most important benefit I can offer Benchley, Faber & Associates is my extensive experience as a buyer of the kind of advertising services you offer. By bringing the perspective of the "account" into the position of account manager, I believe I can contribute significantly to positive client-agency relations.

In addition, my background in design and production enabled me to augment sales at my most recent post by some 35% during my four-year tenure. I developed, produced, and implemented direct mail and newspaper advertising campaigns for an exclusive French import company.

I would like to arrange an opportunity to talk with you further about the position and my qualifications. I may be reached at (630) 555-0228 weekdays and at my home number evenings and weekends. I look forward to hearing from you.

Sincerely,

Ian P. Robinson